Adams Media
An Imprint of Simon & Schuster, Inc.
100 Technology Center Drive
Stoughton, Massachusetts 02072

First Adams Media hardcover edition January 2023

ADAMS MEDIA and colophon are trademarks of Simon & Schuster.

For information about special discounts for bulk purchases, please contact Simon & Schuster Special Sales at 1-866-506-1949 or business@simonandschuster.com.

The Simon & Schuster Speakers Bureau can bring authors to your live event. For more information or to book an event contact the Simon & Schuster Speakers Bureau at 1-866-248-3049 or visit our website at www.simonspeakers.com.

Interior design by Colleen Cunningham

Manufactured in China

10 9 8 7 6 5 4 3 2 1

Library of Congress Cataloging-in-Publication Data
Names: Quinn, Hayley, author.
Title: Do this, not that: dating / Hayley Quinn.
Description: First Adams Media hardcover edition. | Stoughton, Massachusetts: Adams Media, 2023. | Series: Do this, not that | Includes bibliographical references and index.
Identifiers: LCCN 2022014633 | ISBN 9781507219690 (hc) | ISBN 9781507219706 (ebook)
Subjects: LCSH: Dating (Social customs)
Classification: LCC HQ801 .Q56 2023 | DDC 646.7/7--dc23/eng/20220525
LC record available at https://lccn.loc.gov/2022014633

ISBN 978-1-5072-1969-0
ISBN 978-1-5072-1970-6 (ebook)

DO THIS. NOT THAT.

DATING

What to DO (and NOT DO)
in 75+ Difficult Dating Situations

Hayley Quinn

ADAMS MEDIA

NEW YORK   LONDON   TORONTO   SYDNEY   NEW DELHI

To all the team at HayleyQuinn.com.

CONTENTS

4

4 Living Together 118

INTRODUCTION

If you've been doing:

LESS OF THIS:
getting
the dates
you want...

...AND MORE OF THAT:
receiving one
too many "I just
didn't feel the
spark" messages...

Or you wish you were:

DOING THIS:
moving in with a
committed
partner...

...INSTEAD OF THAT:
watching relationships
frequently end up
as a funny story to
tell your friends...

You're in the right place.

For a lot of people, modern dating can feel confusing—
and about as much fun as a job interview. The good news
is that you're *not* stuck being single—*or* always choosing
people who aren't the right fit. You just need a little
guidance in doing *this*—and not *that*—to become better
at dating and relationships!

Do This, Not That: Dating is a straightforward and easy-to-use guide that will help you navigate the world of modern dating, gain the confidence to go after what you want, and create healthy relationships. How exactly? Not by playing any tricks or games, but by focusing on developing your self-esteem, healthy boundaries, and communication skills: the keys for successful dating.

And because dating isn't one size fits all, this book isn't *all* about telling you what to do; rather, it asks you questions and helps you explore your personal experiences so you can make the right choices for *you*. Organized into chapters based on themes like meeting someone you like, getting to know each other, and creating a long-term relationship, you'll identify what to do (and not do) in eighty-one situations, including when:

- 💜 You feel like you never meet anyone you like
- 💜 You can't decide where to go for a first date
- 💜 You're getting more serious and can't agree on whether to have kids
- 💜 You've moved in together and need to figure out household finances
- 💜 You're getting married and your parents don't like your partner
- 💜 Your partner wants to move or get a new job and you feel differently
- 💜 And much more

You're going to understand why things haven't worked out so far, and finally feel ready to build the relationship you deserve! So let's do *this*, not *that*.

HOW TO USE THIS BOOK

Do This, Not That: Dating is your guide to dealing with various difficult dating and relationship situations. It will help you to confidently navigate the ups and downs of meeting people and exploring new relationships. You can dip into this book when you're not sure of what to do in a specific situation; just flip through to the scenario that applies to you. Or, if you want to get your PhD in dating, you can read the book cover to cover.

Each dating scenario is divided into sections—*as seen on the right*—for a comprehensive, actionable guide to handling that situation.

Each scenario is also organized under a main theme of dating, so you can easily find guidance on whatever obstacle you are facing. Whether you are looking to meet someone you like, going on a first date, getting to know someone on a deeper level, moving in together, getting married, or dealing with something in between, there is something for you.

Every decision you make about your dating life is your own; this book will ask you the right questions to help you arrive at the best solution for you. It will guide you in making decisions about the right time to break up with someone, how to deal with a cheating partner, and even how to get more hot dates.

First, you'll find tips for how to deal with the problem at hand.

 Next, you'll explore big no-nos to avoid if you want to date more successfully.

✔ **HERE'S HOW** Then, you'll find clear action steps to tackle the situation, from what to say if, for example, you are feeling really uncomfortable during a first date, to how to have a positive *and* helpful mindset during a difficult time, like when a relationship has ended.

Think This:

This section gives you a mantra for dealing with your dating problem in a way that's calm and confident. If you feel anxious, overwhelmed, or confused, repeat this positive mindset.

Say This:

You can use one of the three example phrases in this section as a model when communicating with your date or partner (or family and friends, in some cases). Choose the phrase that best fits your situation. The advice that's right for you will be based on your individual circumstances. These catchphrases are there to inspire you, but feel free to put them into your own words. Successful dating should never feel like you're reading from a script.

WHAT NEXT?

Once you start thinking about dating in a way that is calm and confident, rather than anxious and overwhelmed, you'll be ready to embrace next steps for moving forward and getting what you want.

Chapter 1

MEETING SOMEONE YOU LIKE

It's the million-dollar question for anyone who's dating: How do you meet someone these days? True, there's a ton of dating apps out there, singles' events, speed dating, matchmaking, etc. Maybe you've tried one, or all, of these without success. The truth is that meeting someone you like is less about *where* you meet someone and more about *how* you go about it; it's not so much *which* dating app you choose, but *how* you use the app.

In this chapter, you'll explore the mental hurdles that can keep you stuck on the starting blocks of dating. Perhaps you never seem to meet anyone you actually like, you're not over your ex yet, or you're terrified of being rejected (again). Whatever obstacle you may be facing, you'll find practical action steps on how to overcome it and get more results in your dating life. You'll create an online dating profile that works, identify a great first message to send, and determine whether you should actually listen to your friends' dating advice. This chapter is designed to help give you the confidence and skills to get out there.

You're Wondering If You're Ready to Date

You'd like to meet someone, but is now really the right time? Maybe it's been a while or you're still hung up on an ex. Then there's how to go about it. It's going to take time, right? You'll (probably) need to use dating apps? You'll need to, *you know*, actually go and meet new people. So how do you know if you're ready to date?

 **DO THIS** *Follow these steps to get started:*

1 **Don't worry about getting your whole life sorted, just some of it.**
Plenty of dating advice will tell you that you have to be happy by yourself first before you're ready to meet a great partner. Yes and no: There isn't an end destination to getting your life together; it's a continual journey. Finding a partner will be a work in progress too. So don't wait for the perfect time. Just start.

2 **Be your own top priority again.**
Dating needs time, and for you to approach it from a place of high self-worth. If you're emotionally drained from a recent breakup, take a time-out. If you're a single parent, consider how you can carve out an evening or two a week where you can focus on finding love. Lots of your best decisions in dating will come when you put yourself first (or equally first, if you have kids).

3 **Create neutral expectations.**
If you go into the world of dating and expect to be swept off your feet tomorrow, chances are you're going to be disappointed. Instead, focus on the basics: You're going to have fun, you're going to meet some new people, and you're going to see what happens.

DON'T LOOK FOR LOVE AT THE WRONG TIME. There are many great times to start finding love, but there are also some bad ones. If you've recently experienced a personal tragedy or a messy breakup, dating can wait. Going on dates to get over someone else never works. Most people have had their fair share of bad breakups, but it's important that you're not still feeling resentful about yours. You want to start dating with a clean slate.

HERE'S HOW

Start with small, motivating steps. If you look only at the big picture (e.g., "I want to get married someday: How? To whom??"), it's going to feel overwhelming. Chunk it down. What do you need to do to get started? You'll need time to meet people: probably quite a lot of people. Later in this chapter, you'll learn how you can get your dating app profile up and running, and also find ideas for how you can meet people in real life. All you need to do is start.

Think This:	**Say This:**
"My immediate goal isn't to fall madly in love. My first goal is to get to know myself better again, to focus on what I'm really looking for in a partner, and to start getting out there!"	"Meeting someone is an important goal for me, so I'm going to make time for it." "This is going to be a journey for me: one where I'm going to learn a lot about myself, meet some new people, and eventually click with someone." "If I haven't made the best choices in the past, that doesn't define me; this time around, I'm doing things differently."

WHAT NEXT?

If you're (mostly) sure you're ready to get started, you're going to need a game plan. In this book, you'll move past some of the most common limiting beliefs that stop you from meeting someone, and find some practical action steps to get started. Don't worry...it might actually be fun!

You Feel Like You Never Meet Anyone You Like

Maybe going on dates is not the problem for you—it's meeting someone you actually like. If you have to go out for drinks with one more person you know you're not attracted to, that's going to suck. It's like all the "good ones" are taken, and you're picking through the leftovers. *Ouch.* Stop right there. There's a huge shift of mindset you're going to need to make to allow yourself to start finding people attractive again.

 *Follow these steps to get started:*

1 **Reexamine your expectations.**
Maybe you have your heart set on there being a "moment" when you meet someone. Maybe you think you'll just know when someone's "The One." But starting today, you're doing things differently. You're going to be challenging your expectations about who you can like.

2 **Change up how you're meeting people.**
If you've found yourself in a dating rut, you need to break your patterns and habits around dating. For example, if you've just been meeting people online, focus on meeting people in the real world for a while. Fed up with going out for drinks? Bring a potential date to a yoga class. If every date feels the same, you need to get some fresh eyes on this.

3 **Give people a chance.**
I know, I know...it's something your great-aunt would say, but it's true! Sure, when you were sixteen you probably felt the spark every five minutes. Now that you're more mature, falling in love might not happen in the same way. If someone seems nice enough, then give them a few dates to really get to know them.

DON'T THINK YOU HAVE A TYPE. Remember: Who you think you like is purely hypothetical. It's an idea. It only becomes a reality when you're arguing over who loads the dishwasher better in a year's time from now. So even if you really think you'll only get along with someone who works in a similar industry, has brown eyes, or shares your love of doubles tennis, prepare to stand corrected!

HERE'S HOW

It's already been established that you need to shake up how you date. If you're going on date after date that all feel the same, you need to give yourself a mental prompt to start evaluating people individually. Try to go on first dates that you'll enjoy anyway, even if there's no spark (this is where that yoga class comes in). Likewise, if your time is very precious to you, do a video call with someone ahead of agreeing to your date, so you can check out the connection before committing further. (And if it's a really bad video call, you can blame the Wi-Fi and get out of there!)

Think This:	**Say This:**
"I might not fall in love in the same way again; love could happen differently for me this time." Your connection could be a grower, not a show-er! Sometimes people really do grow on you. There's more than one way to fall in love. If things haven't worked out before, this could be a great opportunity to do things differently.	"I'm going to get to know them better before coming to any final decisions." "I'm going to learn to date in a way that's rewarding for me, even if there's no spark." "I'm ready to do things differently."

WHAT NEXT? ⟶

Your ability to feel attraction has a lot to do with yourself. So before you write off the whole dating pool as a lost cause, look inward. Can you do things differently? Can you get a new perspective? Can you challenge yourself to date in a different way?

You Think You're Stuck Always Being "The Friend"

It's the classic dating problem: "The people I like never like me." It can be frustrating when you meet someone you click with who only sees you as a friend. If you feel you've spent most of your life walking around in a T-shirt that says "The Friend Zone" on it, fear not; you can change this.

 Follow these steps to get started:

1 Recognize that you put yourself in the friend zone.
You wind up always being the friend because you either don't communicate what you want or you accept less than what you want. There's nothing wrong with being friends if that's something you want. It becomes an issue when you want more but settle for less to keep someone in your life.

2 Get better at communicating your intentions.
If you like someone, you need to let them know. If they tell you that they see you as only a friend, you also need to be radically honest with yourself about whether you can accept this. Does the idea of a friendship with this person make you happy, or will it feel like you're in second place?

3 Stay true to how you want to date.
If you want to find a romantic partner, go on real dates. Don't do hangouts or group things. If someone is interested in you, they will give you time one-on-one. If this doesn't happen, then keep your standards high and be prepared to move on.

DON'T DO NICE THINGS FOR SOMEONE ELSE IN THE HOPE THAT ONE DAY THEY'LL "CHOOSE" YOU. This isn't very nice at all; it's trying to create the circumstances where they feel they owe you a date for all the good deeds you've done. Don't give them all the power to select you as a lover or leave you languishing in the friend zone. Raise your standards. If someone can't commit to you in the way that you want, move on.

 HERE'S HOW

Avoiding the friend zone is a game of two halves. To start with, you need to be prepared to communicate what you want. This can feel scary, as you might feel rejected if they don't want the same things. However, it's a lot less scary than wasting months (even years) hoping that they'll eventually see how great you are together. The other part of this is sticking to your boundaries. If they say they just want to be friends, you have to fully accept it (with *no expectation* for them to change their mind) or move on.

Think This:

"I really liked them, but they're not the only person in the world who I can experience this connection with." This won't be the only time you hear me say this, but there's more than one person you can feel a connection to. Yes, they might be ticking all the boxes on paper, but if they're not willing to meet you halfway, it's a nonstarter.

Say This:

"I respect that, but I can't be just friends with you."

"I think you're great too, but right now, friendship isn't what I'm looking for."

"How would you feel about skipping on 'hanging out' and going for an actual date instead?"

WHAT NEXT?

Don't focus on the occasions where someone you've been romantically interested in has seen you as just a friend. From now on you're doing things differently: You're going to be much clearer about your intentions, and much more honest with yourself about what level of relationship you want to accept. Friendship is a choice that you're going to start to actively make.

The Fear of Being Rejected Is Holding You Back

You'd like to meet new people, but you're terrified of rejection. You're worried that more knockbacks will affect your self-esteem. You feel down because your messages online aren't getting responses. As for speaking to someone in real life...you'd rather go to a job interview. How do you start meeting people when you have an overwhelming fear of rejection?

 Follow these steps to get started:

1 Change how you see rejection.
Everyone faces the possibility of rejection—not just in dating, but in careers and even on social media. When someone doesn't reply to your message or doesn't select you at speed dating, they're not rejecting the entirety of "you"; they're just not experiencing compatibility with the snapshot impression they got of you at that moment. Just because the front cover of the book wasn't exactly what they were looking for, doesn't mean the content of the book is bad.

2 Recognize that everything is a filter.
Start seeing dating as a two-way process. Dating is about discovering mutual compatibility. If they don't respond to your message or are rude when you say hello to them at a party, start to think about whether this is the kind of person *you* would want as a partner.

3 See the opportunity in rejection to learn about yourself.
It may teach you more about what you want in a partner, or give you feedback on what to work on. Dating is also one big communication skills exercise. So if you're not getting many matches, that doesn't mean there's something wrong with "you," but you may want to improve how you communicate who you are online (or in person).

DON'T ENTERTAIN THE BELIEF THAT YOU'RE NOT GOOD ENOUGH. Rejection is an opportunity to see that this wasn't the right person, or opportunity, to experience the love and connection that you deserve.

✓ HERE'S HOW

Stop approaching people (online or offline) with the belief that they have the power to accept or reject you. Don't approach dating like you're applying for a role in their life. Instead, think, "I'm open to meeting new people at the moment, so I'm going to see if we have a connection." If you don't, that doesn't mean there's something wrong with you; it just wasn't a match.

Think This:

"My success with dating isn't about any one person. I need to keep meeting new people until I get that 'click.'" Your goal is to find one of the many great partners out there for you. So don't place too much importance on any one interaction. It's all about the bigger picture of you meeting enough people to find someone(s) that you're compatible with.

Say This:

"I want to create opportunities in my dating life, so I'm going to be curious about getting to know people."

"No one person's opinion of me defines who I am."

"I accept it if someone isn't interested because I trust that there are plenty of people who will be."

WHAT NEXT?

Overcoming the fear of rejection can also be about acknowledging your wins during the dating process. You sent out ten dating app messages this week; great work! You plucked up the courage to ask them out on a date; high five for getting that far! You had a couple of fun dates even if it didn't ultimately work out; that's still good!

You Feel Very Anxious about Dating

Anxiety can wreak havoc in your dating life: it might mean you cancel dates or never have the courage to ask someone out. However, when you know what you're dealing with, anxiety is a lot easier for you to overcome.

 Follow these steps to get started:

1 **Speak to a professional.**
If you notice you're self-sabotaging dates, or frequently need a break from dating because it feels too emotionally intense, these could all be signals that it's not dating that's the issue; it's anxiety. Once you recognize anxiety for what it is, you will be able to start managing it better. To start with, speak to a licensed professional about creating a game plan for managing your anxiety.

2 **Date at your own pace.**
There is no "right" way to date. If you are more comfortable taking things slowly, doing shorter dates, or speaking on the phone, go for it! The best partners for you will be accepting of the pace at which you want to go.

3 **Try an activity date.**
Forget dinner dates! They can be so uncomfortable, especially when you realize you're not attracted to the person before the starters come out. Going on a bike ride together or wandering around a market will give you plenty of conversation starters, and will feel like a less intense way to get to know someone. Likewise, you can try meeting people through shared interests; getting to know someone gradually will help you to relax.

DON'T FOCUS ON ALL THE WAYS THAT THINGS COULD GO WRONG. You'll run out of things to say, other people will be judging you, or you'll like them and then they won't want to see you again. Every time you think of a potentially negative outcome, challenge yourself to think of an equal and opposite positive outcome that you could experience. Perhaps you'll enjoy the conversation, get a compliment on your style, or feel that it wasn't that bad after all. Good things can happen too.

 HERE'S HOW

Stop judging your own needs in dating as somehow "wrong." Yes, some other people may enjoy flirting with strangers, one-night stands, or blind dates, but if none of those things feel right for you, don't panic! Take action in your dating life in a way that feels safe and steady to you. Accept who you are and work with a professional if necessary to help manage your anxiety. You can start small and still reach the end destination that you want.

Think This:

"I'm a catch." Try spending a couple of minutes a day telling yourself why you're someone that another person would be lucky to be with. If you struggle with this exercise, lean on family and friends, and ask them what your good qualities are.

Say This:

"I'm going to go along for thirty minutes, and if I don't feel comfortable, I give myself full permission to leave."

"I'm a catch."

"I'm going to be open to the possibility that this could go right."

WHAT NEXT?

Anxiety can meddle in your day-to-day happiness, but it isn't insurmountable. Once you recognize anxiety for what it is, you can start to manage it so that it doesn't get in the way of all the other amazing things you want to do. You'll also find with a few more experience points on your side that dating stops being this big scary obstacle, and starts becoming an enjoyable part of your life!

You're Not over Your Ex Yet

You met someone you thought was the perfect person, but it didn't work out. Whether your relationship with your ex was too good to be true or chaos from the start, past relationships can cast a long shadow on your dating life. So how do you even start to think about dating when you're not over your ex yet?

 Follow *these steps to get started:*

1 Be realistic about your dating goals.
If you've recently come out of an emotionally intense relationship, dating again can feel strange. Inevitably, no one can compare to that intense connection you felt with your ex. So instead, realign your dating goals. Don't expect to fall madly in love. Expect instead to gradually rebuild your own identity by slowly getting to know new people.

2 Take time out for yourself.
Yes, it's the dating advice no one wants to hear; taking a dating pause can feel like you've been relegated to the backbench of romance. However, this actually isn't the case. The more you get used to this "new single you," the better placed you will be to attract the right future partner.

3 Go cold turkey on your ex.
If you're still creeping on their social media or scrolling back through old photos, this needs to stop *today*. Instead, you really need a clean break. Mute or unfollow them on social media, and if they come up in conversation, simply say, "It just didn't work out." It's time for them to become a bit part (small role) in your life, and for you to remember that you're the main character.

DON'T COMPARE NEW PEOPLE YOU MEET TO YOUR EX.
Yes, your ex might have been smart, successful, and dashingly good-looking, but the fact they're your ex suggests that there was something off in how they related to you. A great relationship isn't made from someone who ticks off boxes on paper; it's about how you work together as a unit. So say goodbye to the possibility of them changing, fall out of love with their potential, and go meet someone who you can genuinely be happy with.

✓ HERE'S HOW

Today you might feel broken-hearted—that there's no way you can ever get over them. And maybe the you of today is hung up on your ex, but trust that you can (and will) grow out of this phase. You are going to mature, adapt, and change as a person, and as you do, your ex will become less and less relevant to who you are. They may well still be important to you, but your relationship with them won't define you, and it won't stop you from finding someone better suited.

Think This:

"Dating isn't like Chutes and Ladders; a breakup doesn't mean I'm back to the start. It means I have the opportunity now to meet someone really good for me." After a relationship breaks down, it can be tempting to think that you're back at square one. That you have to start all over again. You don't. Each relationship will give you a clearer idea of what you want and need. Today you're better placed than ever to know what you need in a future partner.

Say This:

"It just didn't work out."

"I'm excited about the next chapter."

"I'm going to enjoy getting to know myself again."

WHAT NEXT? ⟶

You won't meet the same person again. That is true. However, just because you won't love another person in exactly the same way, doesn't mean you won't love again. You will!

You Don't Think You Have Enough Time to Date

You want to meet someone; it's just finding the time to do it that's the issue. You find yourself forgetting to reply to messages on dating apps for days on end and trying to schedule dates into the next month. How can you meet someone while juggling your other commitments?

 Follow these steps to get started:

1 Ask yourself, "Is this my highest goal right now?"
Dating takes time. If you don't dedicate time to dating, then it's as good as saying you want to get a summer body, while hitting the takeout hard. If you really, *really* want to meet someone, make peace with the fact you're going to have to dedicate time to this.

2 Look for the win-win.
Can you double up on doing something you enjoy that also gives you the opportunity to meet people? Can you swap out the free weights for a body pump class? Learn a foreign language at an in-person event? Meet friends in a buzzy bar as opposed to at your home?

3 Set aside twenty minutes each day to respond to people.
If someone you match with gets one message from you a week, trust me, it will fizzle out. Set aside twenty minutes of your day where you're going to focus on having some back-and-forth on your messages: This should mean you're both more excited to eventually meet.

DON'T GO ON RUSHED DATES. If your attention is 50 percent elsewhere, it will be very hard to click with your date. A lot of your ability to feel the spark comes down to your own frame of mind. You want to be relatively relaxed. You absolutely do not want to be watching the clock from the moment you walk through the door. Nor do you want to routinely cancel dates last minute because "something came up." Start to become the person you want to date.

 HERE'S HOW

Before you commit *a whole hour* to an in-person date, you might want to video chat with someone first to check compatibility. If this isn't working for you, you may need to look at some longer-term lifestyle changes: A job with more flexibility, reliable childcare, or finally finishing your degree might be what you need to start putting yourself first.

Think This:	**Say This:**
"Dating is a top priority for me now, so I'm going to make time for it." Dating isn't always a priority. There are times in your life when other things take precedence. However, if this really is your top goal right now, how can you reprioritize?	"Dating is important to me right now, so I'm going to save time for it." "Instead of feeling overwhelmed and canceling on someone at the last minute, can I choose dates that are easier for me to fulfill?" "Where are some possible win-wins here? How can I use my time in a way that's rewarding and allows me to meet new people?"

WHAT NEXT?

It's time to start saving time! Your immediate goals are to set aside at least twenty minutes a day to focus on this area of your life. Also, promise yourself that you'll start getting better at keeping your commitments. Dedicate time to dating, and your results will change.

You're Not Sure Where to Meet Someone

"Where have all the good people gone?" If your dating life is the equivalent of trying to buy a Christmas present on Christmas Eve ("all the best ones are taken!"), then this is the section for you. If you're confused about which dating app has all the hotties on it or where to meet people in the real world, read on.

 Follow these steps to get started:

1 **Understand it's not about the dating app; it's how you use it.**
Choose an app that suits the style of commitment you want. However, don't fall into the trap of thinking there's one "good app" where all the best catches are: It's about how you interact with the app that makes the difference. Can you filter out people who aren't on the same page as you? Can you create a profile that really speaks to who you want to meet? These are all more valuable questions than, "Which is the best dating app?"

2 **Recognize that you can still meet people in real life.**
Meeting people in person hasn't gone the way of the dodo. You can go out and speak to people at a bar, the gym, or the supermarket (yes, really). And if that all sounds too daunting, then hobbies and interests are a great way to get to know people gradually.

3 **Leverage hobbies and interests that have a built-in social circle.**
If your chosen hobby is stamp collecting, it's unlikely that you'll be able to use it to meet many new people. Ideally, you want to choose a hobby that has a built-in social circle—a tight-knit community with lots of opportunities to socialize. From social dances to running clubs to activism, there are plenty of communities out there for you to tap in to.

DON'T PROCRASTINATE. Procrastination is the enemy of your dating life. Yes, dating can feel like hard work, emotionally exposing, and difficult. It's far too easy to prioritize other things...but if you know that deep down you want to meet someone, you have to start somewhere. As the saying goes, "The best day to start was yesterday, the next best day is now."

 HERE'S HOW

Let go of the idea that there's only one way to meet someone. Be open to all the areas where you could meet someone: Set up a dating app profile (or two), take up a new hobby, ask friends for blind dates, and smile at people during your commute. It all helps.

Think This:

"It's going to happen for me." Get out of the "it's impossible" mindset. If you've spent quite a bit of time telling yourself that it's impossible to meet someone, that no one wants a relationship anymore, or any other kind of defeatist dating rhetoric, now is the time to stop. With a good game plan, you have plenty of time and opportunities to get this right.

Say This:

"Set me up! I'm ready!"

"I'm going to be open-minded as to how and where I'll meet someone I really like."

"People meet one another every day; there's no reason that this can't be me."

WHAT NEXT? ⟶

Stop analyzing, and start doing. When you're starting out at dating, just seeing people you're attracted to (on or offline) is a good start. Take note of all the times you see someone you like and dispel that scarcity myth that all the good ones are taken.

Your Friend Wants to Help with Your Dating Life

Everyone has an opinion as to why you're single. "You're too picky"; "You need to be happy by yourself first"; "You're too nice." You're probably pretty tired of these pearls of wisdom by now! Some friends take this a step further and will hijack your dating apps profile. How can you accept genuine support and weed out the meddlers?

 Follow these steps to get started:

1 Verify your blind dates.
It's oh so painful to hear your friend coo that they've found you "the perfect person" and agree to a blind date, only to be set up with someone you're not attracted to *at all*. Before you commit to a three-course meal, have a low-pressure phone call with your prospective date ahead of time.

2 Trust yourself.
If things haven't been going to plan (to say the least) in your dating life, it can be tempting to divest control of your love life to your friends. Stop asking your friends to ghostwrite your messages. Often it's more valuable to rebuild your self-esteem and start believing that you can do this independently.

3 Be selective about what advice you listen to.
What works well for some people doesn't work so well for others, so get away from the idea that there's one perfect strategy for dating. There isn't. You have to cherry-pick advice. Likewise, if someone insists you're single because "you don't give people a chance," or some other over-simplification of your life, you don't need to heed that counsel. Listen to advice that is empowering and from people you really trust.

DON'T ALLOW A HOSTILE TAKEOVER OF YOUR DATING APPS AND MESSAGES. Letting your friend do it for you sends a message to yourself that you're not capable. By all means, pause dating and strategize, but don't allow yourself to believe that everyone else has got it figured out and that you're a lost cause.

HERE'S HOW

Blind dates can be a good thing: Chances are you'll have shared values, things in common, and (hopefully) they'll be less likely to cancel your date. Some of your trusted friends may also have real insights into your dating patterns and may well be able to shed light on why things aren't working. Just make sure any advice you listen to feels supportive, not judgmental.

Think This:

"There's more than one way to break an egg, and there's more than one way that I can find love." Just because your friend met the love of their life at a salsa dancing class, it doesn't mean that social dancing is the best way to meet someone; it just worked out for them. It's your job to create opportunities for yourself to meet people, and to stay open-minded as to how this might work out for you.

Say This:

"They sound great. I'll give them a call this week and see if we click."

"I like being single, and I'm okay to wait until I meet someone I really click with."

"I know you're saying that because you care, but that advice doesn't resonate with me right now."

WHAT NEXT?

Everyone needs support, and having a group of trusted friends to see you along the journey of single life is a wonderful thing. So before you go on the lookout for a partner, make sure you have some friends, who you love and trust, to high-five you along the journey.

You Need Help Creating a Good Dating App Profile

You're starting to wonder if anyone uses online dating to actually meet someone anymore, or if it's just full of attention seekers and time wasters. How can you create a dating app profile that attracts the people you want to meet?

 **Follow these steps to get started:**

1 Avoid a clichéd profile.
Skip things like, "I like going out and I like staying in," "My friends would describe me as...," or using emojis instead of words. You want a profile that's witty, to the point, and personable. If writing isn't your strong point, dictate your profile: Often people say things in a catchier way than they write them.

2 Choose photos wisely.
You need at least four to six good photos depending on the platform. These photos should be high resolution, and you should be clearly visible in most of the photos. Avoid too many sunglasses, big hats, or pictures of you doing something cool ("Wow, a pyramid!") but where you're very hard to see. Spend some time thinking about the background of your photo (a messy bedroom behind you will make people zoom in on all the wrong details) and the clothes you're wearing (you want to make sure what you're wearing appeals to who you want to date and represents your personality).

3 Figure out your personal brand.
Do you have one photo of you backpacking through Australia and another that's a corporate headshot? Yes, it's good to show that you have a variety of interests, but just be careful that your photos are consistently communicating who you are.

DON'T BE NARROW-MINDED. If you're not getting the results you want online, double-check your criteria for who you match with. Remember: Your perfect type is just hypothetical until you meet someone who you click with, so be prepared to experiment. Someone's level of education can feel very important, but how willing they are to connect with you is more telling.

 ## HERE'S HOW

Blame social media, but there's no doubt that to get ahead in the world of dating apps, you'll need a great profile and especially great pictures. (This doesn't mean you have to be a supermodel, but you will need bright, recent photos that clearly show who you are.) Like all areas of dating, you also have to be proactive at sending messages out and responding to people (more on this in Chapter 2).

Think This:	**Say This:**
"I can meet someone genuine anywhere, I just need to be smart about it." Don't buy into the dating myths that no one wants a relationship anymore. Just like if you walked into a bar, there's a mixed bag online. So keep an open mind, but do your due diligence before making a big commitment to someone you've met on the Internet.	"My photos aren't the best; I need a ring light, a tripod, and a very good friend." "Instead of listing things I like on my profile, how can I describe one experience in detail instead?" "Is my current selection criteria serving me or limiting me?"

WHAT NEXT? ———————————————➤

If your dating app profile isn't currently working for you, don't take this as a reflection on you. Yes, it may be a signal that your storefront (a.k.a. profile) needs some window dressing, but it certainly doesn't mean there's anything wrong with you as a person.

You Don't Know What First Message to Send on a Dating App

Lots of people write nothing on their dating profiles, so being witty can feel challenging. How do you craft a message that can stand out in someone's dating app inbox, without being time-consuming for you?

 **Follow these steps to get started:**

1 Remember that unique is always better.
Sending a message like, "Hey, how's your weekend going?" isn't likely to stand out from the other messages they've received. Always personalize your messages. Look at their profile, pick out a unique detail, and comment on it in a playful way: "What are the chances of me convincing you to swap out your yoga class for boots and a hike?" If you want something generic, at least keep it fun: "So tell me one thing I wouldn't like about you."

2 Follow the motto "half as long and twice as strong."
This means to keep your messages to one or two lines and make them punchy! Consider editing out unnecessary details. Messages also work better when there's one clear item for someone to respond to (e.g., instead of saying, "I like your cat!" try "Do you think your cat would get along with my dog?"). Funny and abstract messages work well: It is about someone reading your message and deciding you'd be a fun person to hang out with.

3 Try an attention-grabbing first word.
Imagine how many messages a person receives that begin with the word "hi" or "hey." Of course, saying "hi" and then their name is slightly better, but experiment with using a more attention-grabbing first word. Try picking something unique to their profile (e.g., "Cookies? Any chance you bring those to first dates?").

DON'T ASK SOMEONE OUT ON THE FIRST MESSAGE. You don't want to seem like you'd want to spend time with them just because they're a pretty face. Instead, asking someone out on a date should be conditional, based on how much they've invested in the interaction.

HERE'S HOW

Like all areas of dating, the name of the game here is to be proactive. Sending likes, winks, and nudges to people is nowhere near as good as a well-crafted first message. If you feel unsure about sending out first messages and would rather be pursued, try sending a low-effort, playful message like, "Can I be cheeky and leave the ball in your court?" This will give the other person the chance to lead the interaction (but still allows you to take initiative).

Think This:

"I want to meet someone, so I'm going to be an opportunity creator in my dating life." People will use online dating for all kinds of reasons. Most people will want to go on a date. Others will be looking for an ego boost after a breakup, or to get more followers on social media. If someone doesn't respond to your message, don't choose to interpret this as them rejecting you. Accept that with dating there's a filtering process.

Say This:

"I'm going to turn off the TV and focus on my messages now."

"They don't have a bio. Does that meet my criteria to message them?"

"Are my messages fun for me to write?"

WHAT NEXT? ⟶

Hopefully this section has given you some inspiration for what makes a great first message. Now that you've got your foot in the door, how do you convert that first message into a date? In Chapter 2, you'll explore how you can move from chatting online to a date, and how to overcome common message problems like your chats fizzling out before they've begun.

You're Dealing with Someone Rude Online

One of the fears you might have about dating apps is that you'll have to deal with rude people. If someone does overstep the mark, how do you handle it and stop it from ruining your dating motivation levels?

 **Follow these steps to get started:**

1 Trust your instincts.
Sometimes it can be hard to specifically pinpoint what someone's doing that makes you feel uncomfortable. In this case, trust your gut instincts; if you're not liking where the conversation is going, get out of there!

2 Keep key details of your life private until you know someone better.
This means no revealing where you live, no meeting for the first time at someone's house, and absolutely no sending money to a stranger online, no matter how convincing their sob story is! No one who is genuinely interested in you will ask you to do any of these things. Most apps also allow you to video chat within the app. This is also handy, as it means you don't even need to swap phone numbers until you're totally convinced that you like and trust this person.

3 Report any dubious behavior.
Dating apps are generally a lot more socially responsible than their social media counterparts when it comes to dealing with harassing behavior. Some, like Match, will even automatically offer to block a user who sends you numerous unanswered messages in a row. Others will let you block a user and send them a warning that they've been harassing you.

DON'T GET INTO AN ARGUMENT ONLINE. As tempting as it can be to try and correct an online troll, or to fight fire with fire, please remember what's at stake here. If someone is being in any way abusive, boundary trampling, or straight-out mean, chances are they're not about to learn from their behavior, even if they receive a real zinger of a message from you. Devote your precious time and energy to better prospects, not trolls.

 HERE'S HOW

Luckily, when it comes to harassment online, the law is gradually shifting in favor of providing better protection for the person being harassed. Yes, some social media companies are still woefully unaccountable when it comes to the safety of their online users, but the law is catching up. In many countries around the world, "cyberflashing" (sending unsolicited explicit images online) is being made illegal. So if you've had a bad experience: Delete, block, and disengage.

Think This:	**Say This:**
"What can I do to not let this one experience define dating for me?" Time to shake off those bad vibes. Don't allow yourself to sink into a negative storyline about dating ("All the good ones are taken," "I only attract the crazy ones," etc.). Instead, remember that this is just one (probably very unhappy) person.	"This doesn't feel right to me, so I'm disengaging." "It's not worth my time and energy to call them out on their behavior, so I will block them and refocus on better opportunities." "Yes, that was a horrible experience, but I'm not going to let it negatively impact how I feel about dating as a whole."

WHAT NEXT? →

You might encounter weird people on dating apps. It is undoubtedly horrible to have an interaction with someone who lacks respect and leaves you feeling violated. However, this is one experience, and it will not be all your experiences. Hit your mental pause button if you're feeling overwhelmed with your recent online encounters, but don't write off dating altogether.

You're Jealous of Friends Who Are Meeting That Special Someone

Is single life starting to feel decidedly less fun? Are your friends slowly getting coupled up? Have they swapped nights out for brunch dates? Do their loved-up pics on social media make you flinch? Here's how to navigate those tricky feelings and be supportive of your friends.

 **Follow these steps to get started:**

1 **Understand that happiness is not a race.**
Just because someone's gotten engaged, had a baby, or reached a life milestone ahead of you, it doesn't mean that they're "all set." Each new phase of life offers different challenges.

2 **Accept new ways of spending time together.**
Yes, nights out may become more challenging once your coupled-up friends start having kids, but that doesn't mean that's the end of your relationship. Go for dinner with them and their partner, or go for a park date with them and their kids. This will help you both to feel less envious and more empathetic toward each other.

3 **Get some new single friends.**
If you feel like the "last one left," single life can soon start to feel miserable, but it doesn't have to be that way. This is just a signal that you need to recruit some new friends who are at a similar stage in life with similar goals. Think of it this way: No one worried about being single at twenty-one; they were all too busy having a great time. Just because some years have gone by doesn't mean you can't recapture this attitude toward single life. Create the social circle you need to keep single life enjoyable and rewarding.

DON'T BECOME A NAYSAYER OF LOVE IN GENERAL. That supportive, loving relationship your best friend has—you want that too, right? Commitment is also kind of a big deal, so it's good to take your time getting there. Keep reminding yourself that you're not in a rush and that there's enough happiness in the world to go around.

HERE'S HOW

Lean into your friendships, even when you're at different life stages. Remember events that are important to them: kids' birthdays, engagement parties, and anniversaries. Celebrate these milestones with them. Also, just because you're not in a relationship right now, it doesn't mean you don't have anything important to share. Help your friends to understand what's significant in your life, so they have an opportunity to support you too.

Think This:

"To achieve the abundance I want in my dating life, I need to cultivate positive feelings about it." If you're sitting on the sidelines (as everyone does at some point) feeling jealous and critical of your friends, you're not getting closer to the love that you want. If you're critical of other people's relationships or convinced that love is a myth, you're only putting a bigger roadblock between yourself and your opportunity to be happy. It's time to love love again.

Say This:

"I just wanted to wish Zach a happy first birthday! I've been thinking about you all; give me a life update."

"Sometimes I find it hard to mention when I need support, as I don't feel it's important compared to other things you've got going on in your life."

"I'm genuinely so happy for you."

WHAT NEXT?

Like the loved-up picture on social media, lean into your friendships and ask for support when you need it. The best friendships will stand the test of different life circumstances. And if other friendships fall away, don't feel too dejected: You now have space to form new relationships.

You're Attracted to Someone at Your Workplace

Familiarity breeds attraction, so having a crush in your workplace is certainly common. But is it a good idea? While many couples might have met through work, should you steer clear of a potentially complicated relationship and focus your efforts elsewhere?

 Follow these steps
to get started:

1 Consider what other channels you are using to meet someone.
Before exploring an attraction in your workplace, consider whether it is possible that you've got a crush on a coworker simply because you're not meeting anyone else. Or maybe you've had a recent breakup and are looking for a distraction? Make sure this isn't coming out of a vacuum of meeting people generally.

2 See if they want to spend time together one-on-one.
If someone is at all interested in getting to know you better, they'll spend time with you one-on-one. So start by suggesting you grab a coffee together at lunch. If they like you too, this will be a no-brainer for them to agree to. It's also low pressure enough to give you both a chance to get to know one another better and, if there's no spark, go back to work with minimal awkwardness. However, even if you get a yes to the coffee, this doesn't necessarily mean they want to date you. So you still need to tread carefully.

3 Evaluate your wider dating goals.
If you're looking for love, and genuinely feel a connection with a coworker, it may be worth exploring. However, if you're just dating casually, there are better places to meet someone. Flings can be fun, but they are in no way worth the trade-off of awkwardness in the workplace.

DON'T KEEP PUSHING IF YOUR EFFORTS AREN'T BEING RECIPROCATED. All successful dating requires reciprocation; if you keep initiating without a positive response, you are walking into dangerous territory. Not only is this demotivating for you, but it could also be considered harassment by them, especially in the workplace. If someone isn't giving you a clear yes, move on.

 HERE'S HOW

So you know that reciprocation is a must for this to work. If they agree to a coffee, use that time to get to know them better. If you're still feeling a connection, suggest going for dinner or drinks sometime. If they appear to be uncomfortable at any time: mission abort! To arrange a meeting outside of work, take their nonwork cell number. Again, if they are hesitant to hand this out, read the writing on the wall; it's not worth making anyone feel uncomfortable.

Think This:	Say This:
"There are a lot of potential people out there who can make me happy." So even if you meet someone at work who seems perfect, remember that they only become a perfect match for you if they're making just as much effort as you are to get things off the ground. If they're not, there's a lot of other people who will, so respect their decision and move on.	"It's been nice getting to know you outside of work. We should get drinks sometime!" "I'm heading out to that new juice place for lunch. Do you want to join?" "I know it's hectic at the moment, so I'll leave you to get back to your work."

WHAT NEXT?

There are probably some very happy couples who met at work. However, this isn't an episode of *Mad Men*, so don't consider the workplace as a potential pickup spot. The harmony of your workplace is far more important than one opportunity for romance.

You're Worried about Ruining a Friendship

You've been looking to meet someone special for a while, and you're starting to think they've been standing in front of you all along. It's a cliché, but could your BFF actually be the person you're supposed to date?

 **Follow these steps to get started:**

1 **Ask yourself if it's really all about them.**
Is it possible that your friend is looking like a better option because you haven't met anyone else exciting recently? Make sure your interest is genuine before taking the next step.

2 **Prepare for handling it if they say they don't feel the same.**
Telling your friend you *like*-like them is a Pandora's box: You can't quite be sure how your relationship with them will be on the other side. You can do your best damage limitation by acknowledging how important their friendship is to you, but you can't guarantee their reaction.

3 **Keep it low-key.**
Avoid spilling the beans on this one when you're drunk, via text, or in a big dramatic statement. Instead, choose a time when you're relaxed and kick-start an open discussion about the possibilities of your friendship, rather than declaring your undying love.

DON'T BROACH THE "I SEE YOU AS MORE THAN JUST A FRIEND" TOPIC WITH A DECLARATION OF LOVE. Conversations like these can feel emotionally intense, and if your friend isn't on the same page as you, it can easily be overwhelming. Instead, aim to be as relaxed and neutral as possible when you speak to them about it. Remember: There should be a limit to how much you can romantically like them before they've committed to the relationship too. Otherwise your romance is just a fantasy.

✓ HERE'S HOW

See if they'll meet you in a more date-like context. If you usually hang out as a group, are they open to spending time one-on-one? If you always catch up after class, will they meet you during the weekend? Open up a dialogue around the possibilities for your relationship (e.g., "Lately, I've wondered..."), rather than put it all on them.

Think This:

"There are many great relationships in our lives and not every one of them is destined to be romantic." It can be confusing when you have strong emotional intimacy with someone and believe it's meant to be something more. However, you also need physical chemistry to create a relationship. So if kissing them feels like kissing a sibling, trust your instincts. Likewise, if they're not open to romance in the same way you are, don't force anything.

Say This:

"Recently I've started to wonder whether this is a friendship, or maybe something more?"

"Exploring things between us has been on my mind."

"I really value our friendship, and respect whatever page you're on with this."

WHAT NEXT?

There are plenty of friends who've realized they actually have great sexual chemistry. So it's not to say that going from friendship to relationship is impossible. In fact, having a partner who is also your best friend is amazing. However, before you take that leap, make sure it's coming from the right place—that you genuinely see potential here, and you're not just looking for a placeholder until you get another hot date.

You Want to Meet Someone IRL

You feel frustrated by the lack of results on dating apps, and you think you'd find it more rewarding to meet someone the old-school way. Your parents may have met at the local roller disco, but does anyone do that anymore? How can you expand your dating options into real life, without coming off as creepy?

 Follow these steps to get started:

1. **Understand that attraction is your reason to approach and connection is your reason to ask for a date.**
   While physical attraction might get you to put one foot in front of the other, have a firm rule for yourself that unless there's a connection (where they're also trying to click with you) you won't be asking them on a date.

2. **Say something personal, but not *that* personal.**
   Physical compliments can easily come off as too much. The other person may feel objectified and uncomfortable. So instead choose to say something personal but not in any way explicit. "I like that you're reading a real book," "I like how you're always smiling," and "I like how confidently you walked in just now."

3. **Look out for reciprocation (there's that word again) from them.**
   Say hi at an airport (it could be so romantic!), and someone might be unsure how to respond. Don't get too far ahead of yourself without checking in with them that they seem comfortable. They should be in no rush to leave the conversation, offering some information about themselves (read on for more of a step-by-step guide on this) and making eye contact. If they appear uncomfortable, get out of there! You need to invest your time in people who are open to the same things as you.

DON'T ASSUME EVERYONE SEES THINGS THE SAME WAY.
Some people would be all up for meeting a date at the gym—others will feel like that's their sacred workout space. Before you know what someone is comfortable with, proceed with caution. Avoid physical compliments ("you've got great legs"...ah!) and don't keep pushing if someone is at all hesitant.

 HERE'S HOW

So let's imagine you've started the conversation: Where do you go from here? A good first litmus test of someone's comfort level is to swap names. If they don't reciprocate, wish them a good day and exit stage left. If they do reciprocate, share some more information about yourself. This sounds counterintuitive, but giving the other person some background information on you will help them to trust you more. "I don't know about you, but my friend from work dragged me here tonight; I live over on the other side of town" doesn't sound particularly clever, but it imparts a lot of information to the other person about who you are.

Think This:	**Say This:**
"I need a good intention to approach someone." Instead of thinking "OMG I'm flirting with them!" change your mindset to: "I'm curious about them," "I'm going to make their day," or "I'm just going to see what they're about."	"Hi, I know I'm gate-crashing your night out, but I just had to say…"

"I like how you are [insert something unique they're doing]."

"I don't know about you, but I [tell them something about yourself to put them at ease]." |

WHAT NEXT? ⟶

A lot of the success of meeting someone in real life isn't about how smart, funny, smooth, or confident you are: It's about whether they want the same things.

Chapter 2

GOING ON A FIRST DATE

First dates should be exciting and fun, right? But maybe yours are currently feeling more like a job interview. And while it would be nice if the next person you went on a date with was "The One," this might not be entirely realistic. Chances are you'll be going on quite a few first dates before you meet someone you truly click with. On some dates you'll know after approximately two seconds that you're not attracted to them; other times, you might feel a huge spark and not know what's the right next step.

This chapter is all about helping you to stay motivated (and enjoying yourself) through these early dates, and how to show up on your dates as your best self. You'll learn how to tackle common first-date conundrums like how to split the bill and how to leave if you are feeling uncomfortable. You'll find practical tips for improving your conversation skills and learning why a silence doesn't always have to be awkward. Feeling like your first dates go well, but then the other person never seems to want a second date? You'll also explore examples of what to do when their messages the next day seem distant. As you read on, remember that a first date isn't about you being accepted or rejected by the other person: It's a two-way compatibility exercise, to figure out who is a great match for you.

You Want to Ask Someone Out

Whether you've been chatting to someone online, went up to them in a bar, or skated across an ice rink toward them, there comes a time when you're going to want to ask them out on a date.

 *Follow these steps to get started:*

1 Make it clear it's a date.
Don't suggest you "organize a group thing" or "help them with that project." Comments like this create a one-way track toward unmet expectations and disappointments. Don't suggest "hanging out some-time": Be direct and invite them on a date.

2 Keep what you're asking for small.
The first thing you want to ask for is their number or social media handle. Try saying this assertively ("Let me grab your number") and avoid saying, "Let me grab your number, and then I'll give you a message next week and maybe we can go for dinner?" Did you notice how that request just got bigger and bigger? Get their contact details first before diving into date planning.

3 Only ask them on a date if they're also making an effort.
If you're messaging someone online and their whole chat has consisted of "lol" and "I guess so," do not ask them out! Remember: No connection, no date! If they're not putting any effort in, and you're still trying to date them, you will come across as someone who's more of a chancer than a chooser in dating.

DON'T ASK SOMEONE OUT IN A FIRST MESSAGE. No matter how great their dating profile looks, you don't know them enough to love them! If your current messages to a person are being met with tumbleweeds, don't keep rewarding their lack of response with more suggestions about how you could spend time together. Take the feedback loop that they're just not into you and move on.

 HERE'S HOW

To make a date suggestion sound (dare I say it) smooth, try and tie it into the overall conversation. For instance, if you've been talking about travel, you could say, "Morocco might be a bit ambitious for a first date; can we do mint tea here instead?" What you want is for the other person to agree in principle to your suggestion for a date, and after that you can firm up the logistics.

Think This:	**Say This:**
"I'm not going to wait forever." There's an opportune moment here for you to make your move. If your intention is to meet someone to date, you don't want to become their long-term pen pal instead. At some stage you need to check out whether they're open to the same things as you or not. Leave it too long and the interaction will fizzle out. If someone can't take this next step with you, then you need to redirect your focus elsewhere.	"In case we don't bump into each other again, let me get your number." "A conversation this weird warrants an in-person meeting." "Gotta love a fellow bookworm. What's your schedule like next week?"

WHAT NEXT? ⟶

If someone is genuinely interested, they will give you a clear yes when you ask them out. If you get hit with a barrage of "maybe more toward the end of the month," "I've just got to get this paper in!" or "I might be free Tuesday at 4 p.m. for an hour—I'll let you know," they're just not that interested. Focus your efforts on people who give you a "Heck yes!" not an "Err, maybe."

Someone Asks You Out, but You're Not Interested

Ah, this is awkward. Despite really, really wanting to meet someone special, you've just been asked out by someone you're not attracted to. You might be cursing your inability to "see them in that way," but the result is the same: You need to let them down gently.

 Follow these steps to get started:

1 Make it a clear "No, thanks."

It can be tempting to make up an excuse to spare their feelings. You might want to blame a work deadline, family commitments, the fact your dog needs a haircut...and hope that they get the message. The problem is, some people *won't* get the message and will check in with you a week later. This is when things can get awkward, and also the other person can feel seriously misled. People won't like a rejection, but they'll much prefer a clear and kind "no" to feeling strung along.

2 Use this as an opportunity to reassess your type.

Before you turn down this person's offer, you might want to check in with yourself as to why it's a no from you. Do you get that "icky" feeling when you think about kissing them? Or is it that you promised yourself that you'd never go out with someone named Tom ever again? Make sure your criteria for a date is in the right place.

3 Don't endlessly tolerate unwanted attention if they keep asking.

Provided you give a clear "no" to someone, they should really stop asking. If someone keeps asking, cajoling, and attempting to convince you to go out with them, it isn't romantic—it's boundary pushing, and a big red flag. Don't feel bad if you need to hit "delete, block."

DON'T GHOST PEOPLE. Everyone hates it. You may hate conflict and not want to hurt their feelings, but this lack of closure can feel disorientating for the other person. They'll end up overanalyzing their every move and wondering where things went wrong. Being direct here takes courage, but most people will respect you for it.

 **HERE'S HOW**

People are more resilient than you think. They hate being ghosted but will be okay with a clear response that lets them know where they stand. (And remember: If they're not okay with it, this just underlines the fact that you made the right call!) Try saying something like, "Thank you for last night, but I want to be upfront with you that I didn't feel a romantic connection."

Think This:	**Say This:**
"I'm not going to fear letting this opportunity go, because I trust another will come along." You want to aim to make your dating decisions from a place of self-esteem, not one of fear. You don't need to convince yourself to like someone because you're worried that they're the only option you're going to get. Nor do you need to say yes to a date just because you're worried that you'll let someone down. Go on dates because you feel excited about them.	"I appreciate the compliment, but I don't feel we have a romantic connection." "I want to be honest with you that I didn't feel enough of a connection to continue." "I can't commit to that, as I wouldn't want to mislead you about what I can offer you."

WHAT NEXT?

Every time you say yes to something, you always say no to something else. There's an opportunity cost to everything. So save that time, energy, and motivation for dates that you really want to go on.

You're Feeling Nervous about Meeting Them

If right now you'd rather go to a job interview than a first date, there are strategies you can use to feel calm and confident about meeting someone new.

 Follow these steps to get started:

1 Change your mindset: Become the interviewer, not the interviewee.
A lot of first-date stress comes from a fear of being judged by the other person. Will they like you? Will they accept you? Instead of going into a date wondering how you can become the perfect person for them, you need to focus on what *you're* looking for in a potential partner.

2 Give yourself plenty of time to get to the date.
There are also some simple action steps you can take to feel calmer about your date. If you need to make a sprint finish to your date or get held up in traffic, this will just add to the pressure! A rushed date is never a good date. Plan your travel (and your outfit) in advance, so you can turn up on time and relaxed.

3 Tell them how you feel.
There's a way that you can express to someone that you feel nervous while still coming across as confident (really). Vulnerability also gives someone the chance to empathize with you. Try saying something like, "I'm glad I was on time; traffic was crazy, and I was already a little nervous about meeting you." Verbalizing how you're feeling will also often help you to feel better. You may be surprised that the right people will like you even more for opening up.

DON'T FIXATE ON EVERYTHING BEING PERFECT. Don't try to memorize witty things to say, or go over the date in your mind before you're sitting down in front of them. You're not there to put on a perfect performance in the hope that they like you. It's actually better for you to be present and have a clear idea in your mind of what qualities you'd like to see in them. Accept that sometimes you'll click with someone, and sometimes you won't, and that's okay. The bigger picture isn't about getting this one date to like you; it's about finding the right matches for you.

HERE'S HOW

Experiencing fewer first-date jitters starts with feeling good in yourself. Take some time out before your date for some self-care. And try to avoid that "it will steady my nerves" pre-date glass of wine; you want a clear head to know if you're really connecting with your date or not. Also avoid overcommitting yourself, squeezing dates into time slots that you know are going to be hard for you to keep. Don't agree to dates that you know are going to be exhausting for you to travel to. In short: Make it easy for yourself.

Think This:

"I feel really excited about where I'm at with dating." There's a fine line between feeling nervous and feeling excited about something. Start seeing the butterflies in your stomach as a sign of positive anticipation rather than all-consuming nerves.

Say This:

"I've got a confession to make… I was actually a little nervous about meeting you today."

"I'm excited to meet you too."

"I want to meet you, but I don't want to rush our date. Can we rain check until next week?"

WHAT NEXT? ⟶

Start building a deep trust within yourself that you are good enough. Go on dates that you can enjoy anyway, even if there's no connection. Stop blaming yourself if things don't progress to a second date: It's not all on you to impress them; they have to meet you halfway!

You Want to Be Safe on a First Date...Even If You're Excited

What's an ingredient to romance that you might not have thought about? Trust. For you to feel the spark, you first need to feel safe. This is especially true when you're meeting someone in person who you've only spoken to online before. How do you date safely?

 Follow these steps to get started:

1 Always meet in a public space.
This sounds obvious on paper, but if you like someone, and they're being very persuasive about you coming over to their home, it's a principle that you may forget. It's rare, but people can pose online as someone they're not; so even if you're seriously savvy, always meet in a public place.

2 Tell someone you trust where you're going.
Another first-date basic is to keep someone you trust in-the-know about your plans. This can also help hold you accountable to checking in with them to verify that you are okay. Some apps also track your location, so consider sharing this in real time with a good friend.

3 Consider a pre-date video or phone call.
Yes, good banter on messages can help you to connect, but nothing beats hearing someone's voice to figure out whether you'll get on in the real world. Be wary if someone doesn't want to talk on video or the phone, or their "Wi-Fi keeps failing" at just the moment when you call. Someone genuine should be open, transparent, and easy to get a hold of.

DON'T GO FASTER THAN YOU'RE COMFORTABLE WITH. Your gut instinct often knows best. If someone feels too forward, or a comment they made doesn't ring true, listen to your feelings. Also notice how accepting someone is of your personal boundaries. For instance, if you've expressed that you're going home by yourself tonight, and someone keeps trying to change your mind, that's a red flag!

 HERE'S HOW

On top of listening to your instincts, you can also check out a potential date online. This is a fine balance: Overanalyze their every social media post and you may create an idea of who they are in your mind that doesn't give you a clean slate to meet them in person. However, the Internet is your friend for confirming the basics that someone is who they say they are.

Think This:

"Getting to know them is a process that can't be rushed." Accept that it takes time to get to know someone; go at your own pace. Someone can seem perfect on a first date, but don't take this as set in stone. Avoid thinking "We're just so similar" without doing your due diligence in real life to get to know them. And remember, you don't know them yet, so always base your decisions about how fast you're going to take things on that fact.

Say This:

"Can we start with a video call this weekend?"

"Cocktails sound great… but can we kick-start with a coffee?"

"Sharing my location now. I'll message you when I get home."

WHAT NEXT?

Do dates that are easy for you and don't put sticks of dynamite under your comfort zones. It's perfectly okay to be assertive when it comes to suggesting a first-date venue, or saying that you'd like to talk on the phone before you meet. Remember: Anyone who is on the same page as you in terms of what they want will happily agree to date at your pace.

You Need to Decide Where to Go on a First Date

You want to have a great first date, but isn't going out for dinner a little old-school? "Grabbing drinks" can also feel a bit blah—and is a coffee date too friendly? You can't kiss someone in Starbucks, right? Read on for a short guide to picking out a first-date venue that's perfect for your dating goals.

 *Follow these steps to get started:*

1 Plan your dates.
No one likes an unplanned date. A "let's go wander around and see what we like" doesn't make the other person feel cared for, and it's hard to get excited about a plan that vague. Have a clear plan for a venue or start point for your date.

2 Make it easy for the other person to agree to.
It's usually smart to start with a date that's easy for the other person to commit to. Tickets to a concert or a trip to Paris may sound awesome on paper, but in reality, the other person will just panic that it's going to get awkward. A one- to two-hour date is a good sweet spot to get to know one another, with an escape in sight if things get uncomfortable.

3 Instead of thinking of the perfect date for them, think about what kind of date you'll enjoy.
Especially if you feel like you're in a rut with dating, and motivation is thin on the ground, it can be smart to suggest a date based around your hobbies and interests (e.g., a bike ride, a yoga class, etc.). Likewise, if you find first dates nerve-wracking, an activity date where you're moving around can feel less intense than sitting opposite one another at a table.

DON'T OVERCOMMIT YOURSELF IN ANY WAY. There's no guarantee this first date will lead to a second, and an easy way to feel bad is if you've overspent your money or your time. Stick to dates that are comfortably within your budget, and don't travel miles out of your way to meet someone or hang out with them for ten hours straight. Give as much of yourself as you are comfortable with, knowing there's no guarantee that you'll meet again.

✓ HERE'S HOW

Extending a date is a lot easier than bailing out: Start with a non-ambitious first date. A walk around somewhere scenic with a couple of iced lattes can turn into a lunch date if you feel a click. However, to make it easy for the other person to commit to, and easy for you to excuse yourself if you're not feeling it, stick with a low-key first date.

Think This:	**Say This:**
"It's okay for me to be assertive about my preferences." If your date suggests meeting somewhere that's inconvenient for you, don't be afraid to make a counter-suggestion—just be nice about it. There's no pressure for you to meet at the bar next to their apartment block.	"Can we meet halfway? I don't cross the river for anyone ;-)."
	"How about we grab some iced coffees and take a walk by the canal?"
	"I know the best place for hot chocolates if you're game?"

WHAT NEXT? ⟶

Yes, try to choose a date that's unique enough to show you've put some thought into it, but stay focused on choosing a date where you'll feel comfortable, have fun, and won't feel overcommitted.

You Can't Figure Out Who Pays

Splitting the bill is one of dating's most contentious questions. Is it on the person who invites you to pay the bill? In heterosexual encounters, should it always be the guy who pays? What happens if you get to the end of the date and realize that your date isn't even going to offer to split the bill?! So how do you navigate your dates and stay on budget?

Follow these steps to get started:

1 **Accept that there is no "right" answer here.**
Yes, it's annoying when there isn't a golden rule that everyone can just follow. However, the "right" answer to who splits the bill does come down to personal preference. Some people will enjoy being the provider and paying, others will find it attractive when someone treats them, and some will feel comfortable only with an equal split. Your goal is to decide what your viewpoint is and then seek out people who are complementary to you.

2 **Understand your role as the person who chose the date.**
If you choose the venue, there might be an expectation for you to split the bill. If you are the person who's responsible for date planning, and you suggest a specific restaurant or bar, the other person *might* assume that because it's your choice, it's your treat. Assumptions in dating are a good way to wind up unhappy, but bear this assumption in mind when you're suggesting a date.

3 **Stick to dates that are firmly within your budget.**
A good date doesn't need to be fancy! You can show just as much thoughtfulness taking someone to your favorite cozy café, which makes incredible smoothies, as you can going to an upscale restaurant. You also want to go on dates that make you feel comfortable, and knowing that you're about to be hit with a big bill is one way to feel really uncomfortable.

DON'T ASSUME YOUR DATE IS GOING TO PAY. In fact, don't assume much about your date at all. Even if they've chosen the venue and are "leading" the dating experience, at the end of the date you should offer to split the bill. Or get a round of drinks. Or dessert. Or anything that shows your intent to contribute to this experience.

HERE'S HOW

Start with a first date that is a low-investment option for you both: a round of drinks or a coffee will allow you to not only establish whether there's a connection, but also whether you're both on the same page about splitting the bill. Remember that your goal here is to find someone who has a similar outlook to you; do this when the stakes are low!

Think This:

"This is really a question of compatibility." Some couples will happily divide everything at exactly 50 percent, some will operate on a "you get this one, I'll get the next one" policy, and others will have one person who likes to pay and one who likes to receive. There's no perfect way of dividing it up; it comes down to what your relationship values are.

Say This:

"Put that card away; it's my treat."

"Thank you so much for dinner; drinks are on me."

"What do you say we split this fifty-fifty...sound fair?"

WHAT NEXT? ⟶

Compatibility is a complicated equation: Splitting the bill, political views, sexual chemistry...there are hundreds of small things that make us click with someone, or not. Don't second-guess your beliefs too much, and instead look for someone who shares them.

You're Not Sure How to Get a Good Conversation Going

Are you terrified of awkward silences, running out of things to say, or bombarding your date with questions? If you want to build a genuine connection and dodge the "I just didn't feel the spark" messages, you need good conversation skills. In this section you will learn how to get better at talking to someone you're attracted to.

 **Follow these steps to get started:**

1 Ask questions you care about.
Yes, asking, "So how far away is that?" isn't going to set anyone's world on fire. Instead, focus on big questions that allow you to explore someone's personality; for instance, "So who's your best friend, and would I like them?" is a great way to understand what their values are. Questions that create hypothetical scenarios you can discuss ("If we'd met five years ago would we have clicked?") can also work well. Questions that allow you to learn something about them ("So what's one thing I'd have never guessed about you?") are another example of good questions that will enable you to build a connection.

2 Talk about yourself.
When too much of the conversation's focus is on the other person, they can feel put on the spot. Being candid is a necessary step to give context about your life that allows the other person to trust you.

3 Take a risk.
Share your dark sense of humor, be candid, talk to them as if you're already good friends. This will help your conversation to be more engaging, and if they don't like your jokes, perhaps they're just not compatible with you.

DON'T STICK TO SMALL TALK. Small talk keeps you stuck on a superficial level of conversation. You talk about stuff, rather than exploring how you relate toward one another. Unless you get a little more personal with someone, neither of you will be able to judge if a connection is possible. You might get stuck discussing sofa cushions when you could have fallen in love!

 HERE'S HOW

It's not what you talk about; it's how you talk about it. For example, talking about work can be boring (especially when you're on the "so how long have you worked there for?" track), but it could also be exciting if instead you'd asked, "So what motivated you to get started there?" Get away from this idea that there's better and worse topics of conversation; all topics of conversation are an opportunity to get to know the other person.

Think This:

"I can talk easily to people; I just need to facilitate myself speaking openly when I'm attracted to someone." If right now you worry that conversation skills don't come easily to you, chances are it's not that you're bad at conversations—it's that you need to learn to apply your good conversation skills to your dates.

Say This:

"What could I learn about this person that would make me more attracted to them?"

"What do I love to talk about?"

"How can I give myself permission to be more candid on my dates?"

WHAT NEXT? ⟶

Go into a conversation trying to create a perfect script that will impress someone, and you won't get very far. Go into a conversation focused on what you want to understand about them and express about yourself, and you'll stand a far better chance of connecting.

You're Trying to Decide How Personal Is Too Personal

Everyone has a different preference for how open they want to be with someone they've just met. Some people will be discussing acne and first loves within minutes of meeting one another; others will prefer getting to know someone more slowly. It's a balance: By being open, you help to build a connection, but overshare, and you could scare them off.

 Follow these steps to get started:

1 **Ask questions that allow the other person to set the pace.**
When you ask a discursive question like, "So what's one thing I wouldn't like about you if we got to know each other better?" you give the other person an opportunity to set the pace of the interaction. The other person can choose to answer in a way that's flirtatious, closed off, or neutral. How they respond will give you an indication of how comfortable they feel being open with you.

2 **Add a caveat to what you're saying to show you're socially aware.**
You may hesitate to share that dirty joke you think is hilarious, or make that controversial comment because you're not sure how it's going to be received. But being opinionated, and showing the real you, often makes for a good date, so go for it—just add a caveat to prepare the other person for what they're about to hear: "You may think I'm crazy for thinking this, but…"

3 **Pay attention to them.**
People give you all the clues you need in a conversation as to what they're comfortable with. Is their body language relaxed? Are they smiling and engaged? Or have they just folded their arms and checked the time on their phone? Listen not just to people's words but their body language cues when judging how comfortable they seem.

DON'T ASK INTERROGATORY QUESTIONS. Asking someone how many sexual partners they've had isn't going to make either of you feel good. Instead of jumping in to ask this question, stop yourself and question what your intention behind asking it is. Are you secretly looking for reassurance that they're genuinely interested in you?

 HERE'S HOW

Like so many areas of dating, there's no clear-cut rule for how personal is too personal; it's going to come down to individual preferences about how much someone wants to open up. This also links to compatibility: If you're a frank communicator, you may find yourself feeling frustrated if the other person appears closed off or secretive. Likewise, if you have a strong sense of when is and isn't an appropriate time to talk about something, you may find that dating someone who's candid destroys the mystery. If your date's on a totally different page than you, it may just not be a match.

Think This:	Say This:
"No one comes with a user manual. Opening up is my chance to share with someone what's important to me." In order for people to understand and accept you, you need to be open about what makes you tick. Do this at a pace that feels comfortable to you, and if it's hard for you to be vulnerable, you may want to share that!	"I think that's more of a fourth-date question!" "I'm an open book, so just stop me if I'm going too fast for you." "I probably shouldn't confess to this on a first date, but…"

WHAT NEXT? ⟶

Go into dates with the intention to be open, but also with the intention to listen. If your date can't quite match your pace for disclosure, or if you feel they can't respect your boundaries to slow it down, this is telling you something about your compatibility.

You're Feeling Really Uncomfortable and Want to Leave

You're aware you've only been on the date for twenty minutes, but your gut instinct is telling you loud and clear to get out. How do you leave quickly without this getting any worse?

 **Follow these steps to get started:**

1 Trust your instincts.
You don't need a specific reason to feel the way you do; accept how you feel and trust your instincts. If you want to leave, leave. The reason(s) why you felt so uncomfortable will probably become clear when you've had some time to reflect on the date.

2 Let people know you feel uncomfortable.
You will start to feel safer if you can let someone know that you feel uncomfortable. It could be that you message a friend for some emotional support or tell a member of staff that you feel unsafe. In some bars, if you ask for an "Angel Shot," it lets the bartender know you are looking for help. In the UK, asking for "Angela" can tip off waitstaff to your discomfort. Learn more about distress signals in your area online.

3 Make a judgment call about how honest you want to be about your reason for leaving.
If you feel safe, just uncomfortable, you may find it empowering to be direct and say, "I want to be open that I don't think we're connecting, so I'm going to leave." If, however, you feel at all unsafe, you don't need to be this candid. You can either make an excuse (you're unwell, your roommate is locked out, etc.) or you can say that you've realized that you're not ready to date. Don't feel a need to be open if you feel unsafe.

DON'T BE PUSHED OUTSIDE YOUR COMFORT ZONES. If your date is very persistent about giving you a ride home or wants you to stay at their house, watch out. Anyone sincere, with healthy boundaries, will be able to accept a no the first time they hear it. If you're not comfortable, don't worry (not even for one second) about being rude, just leave. This doesn't mean it's a no forever from you, but give yourself space to think it through.

✔ HERE'S HOW

You may have a mixture of feelings about leaving a bad date: angry, indecisive, or guilty for not staying longer. While it's important to be considerate of someone else's feelings, respect your own limits and exit a date if you feel uncomfortable.

Think This:

"I notice I'm feeling uncomfortable a lot during dating. Could there be an underlying reason for this?" If feeling uncomfortable on a date is a recurring theme for you, then you may also want to check in with yourself about how much anxiety dating is causing you. If you think it's less about the people you're meeting, and more about just meeting new people in general, social anxiety may be the underlying issue here. Reach out to a licensed therapist to develop coping strategies.

Say This:

"I've got to go; my room-mate is locked out."

"I've realized I'm not ready to date right now, so I'm going to leave."

"Can I have an Angel Shot, please?/Can I please speak to Angela?"

WHAT NEXT? ⟶

If it's a question between disappointing your potential date or listening to your boundaries, always prioritize looking after yourself. If you stay on a date that's making you feel really uncomfortable, you risk having an experience that puts you off dating in the longer run. It's not about this one date; it's about you staying motivated and comfortable meeting new people.

You're Not Sure Whether to Kiss on a First Date

You think there's a spark (finally!), but on a first date should you lean in for a kiss? It's another one of those "there's no rule here" parts of dating. Some people will find that kissing on a first date is a natural next step; here are ways you can initiate a kiss without alienating the other person if they're not on the same page as you.

 Follow these steps to get started:

1 Have some physical contact.
You may not intuitively know how much spark you could have with someone. By testing the water with a hug, linking arms, or, yes, maybe a kiss, you could get important feedback about your physical chemistry.

2 Use kissing to signal your intentions.
You may not want to kiss on the first date, but if you want this to be a romantic relationship, then you'll probably want to kiss them at some point. If you don't make your move, this could miscommunicate to them what your intentions are. Instead of giving both of you the opportunity to romantically connect, this interaction could fizzle.

3 Choose a moment that's conducive to kissing.
Often if you wait until the end of your date, you'll find yourself standing outside a bus depot, or a subway platform, or somewhere equally unromantic to make your move. If you think you'd like to kiss your date, choose a venue that will help you to find your moment. Sitting side by side at a bar makes the mechanics of kissing a lot easier than when you're sitting opposite one another at a table (try leaning across it...awkward!). If you've gone for a daytime date, look out for a strategically placed park bench!

DON'T KISS THEM OUT OF THE BLUE. First-kiss attempts only ever go badly (like if your date lunges backward, terrified) if there's no communication before the kiss that it could happen. Start with smaller touches: Are they happy with you touching them on their arm? Leaning in? If your date is happy, receptive, and tactile, then this is a good sign, but make sure you verbalize your intentions before going in for the kiss.

 HERE'S HOW

Gone are the days of having to intuit when's the right moment for a kiss. Asking for consent is sexy. You can cut out the guesswork and show that you respect their personal boundaries by communicating what you want. If you look someone in the eyes and say, "So can I kiss you now?" or "I'd like to kiss you now," you're being clear, confident, and seeking agreement before making your move.

Think This:

"This is what I feel is the right moment; let me check in with them to see if they feel the same." If they're not on the same page as you right away, it doesn't mean a kiss is never going to happen. If someone doesn't reciprocate wanting to kiss in that moment, acknowledge it in a lighthearted way. Ironically, if you handle their "not just yet" well, they may find themselves more attracted to you.

Say This:

"Darn, I thought I'd picked my moment then!"

"You're so far away! Can I move my seat over?"

"I like you, and I'm really enjoying our date. I just want to take my time getting to that stage."

WHAT NEXT?

A kiss isn't a contract, so don't assume because you've kissed that you'll see them again or that there's any implied exclusivity: This is just the start of getting to know them.

You Really Like Them...Now What?

It's been a successful date: However, you're not quite sure what to do next. Should you suggest a second date or wait for them to ask? Send them a thank-you message, or is that too much? Uh-oh...no sooner have you established that you like someone than you start to second-guess exactly what you should do next.

 Follow *these steps to get started:*

1 **Send a thank-you message or respond to theirs.**
If your goal is to have a stable, loving relationship, then you don't need to play games like pretending you're not that interested in them. Instead, you should be looking to openly communicate, and see if they reciprocate. Sending a "Thanks for tonight, I had a good time" message isn't too much, and allows you to check in with them about how they're feeling.

2 **Suggest a second date—organically.**
It's good to be clear about what you want, but before you organize logistics for date number two, have some dialogue. Otherwise, the exchange might feel transactional. You may want to "lock it down," but have faith in yourself that they feel the same; you don't need to rush this next step.

3 **Remember that it's (very) early days.**
It's refreshing to have a great date. In fact, you may have gone months without meeting anyone you liked this much. However, a first date is really someone's highlights reel. It shows you that you're attracted to them, that you have some personal chemistry...and that's about it. There's a lot you still need to figure out about them to understand whether you might work out longer term. So keep your feet firmly on the ground and be aware of all you've still got to discover about them.

DON'T BE TOO DISAPPOINTED IF THEY DON'T FEEL THE SAME. If they're not willing to explore the relationship with you, that tells you they're not one of the many right people for you. So take them at their word, recognize that the vital ingredient of willingness was missing here, and move on.

HERE'S HOW

If it's working, it should feel easy. Even if you felt a spark, if they're noncommittal about a second date, this is probably a nonstarter. Good relationships are characterized by ease; things should generally flow. So don't worry about getting the timing perfect for suggesting a second date; if you're compatible and have similar relationship goals, it should be easy to arrange another date.

Think This:

"I like them but there's a lot I've still got to discover about them." Don't go down the "we're just so similar and they're perfect for me!" route. Yes, it was a great first date, but before you emotionally overcommit to the idea of them, remind yourself of everything you don't know about them yet. Stay objective and remember that getting to know someone takes time.

Say This:

"I like them so far, but let's just see how things go."

"It would be great to see you again—what's your schedule looking like next week?"

"I just might have had a good time too ;-)"

WHAT NEXT?

A lot of people get stuck between the first date and the second date. If you're consistently not getting second dates, it's worth thinking about how you act on first dates: Are you being authentic, or putting on a show? Are you playful, relaxed, and emotionally warm to spend time with? Are you open about when you're attracted to someone? If they're not feeling the spark, troubleshoot this issue by asking these questions.

You Didn't Feel a Spark and Aren't Sure about Another Date

They took you on a nice date. They dressed nicely. In fact, just about everything about them was nice...but you're not really feeling it. If someone's doing all the right things, but you're not feeling the spark, what do you do?

 Follow these steps to get started:

1 **Go on another date that's different than the first.**
There's no harm in going on a second date. Or a third. As long as you're not declaring your undying love, and are being open that you just want to see how things go, you are allowed to explore if there's any potential here. If you're shutting down opportunities very early on based on a snap judgment, you're probably not giving yourself the best chance of really connecting with someone.

2 **Challenge how important the spark is to you.**
Do you need that "butterflies in your stomach" feeling to want to see someone again? Would you feel like your relationship is somehow less good if you didn't get the feels? What qualities (if any) are more important to you in someone than the spark?

3 **Remember that they're not the only person who has good qualities.**
Yes, they're kind, caring, and smart...but so are a lot of other people. Don't make this decision harder on yourself by somehow imagining that this is your only chance to be with someone who has those qualities. If they're great on paper, but something's missing for you, use this as an opportunity to set a new benchmark for yourself about how you deserve to be treated.

DON'T RUSH A DECISION. After the first date you might feel intense pressure to immediately decide whether you like someone. The thing is, first dates only give you a very limited snapshot of a person to work with. So even if you feel like you like someone, you might just like your first impression of them. Give yourself some time here to explore your connection and form a genuine impression of them.

 HERE'S HOW

Could it be a grower, not a show-er?! Love doesn't always come in the same form. You may have only had feet-sweeping romances before, but if they haven't worked out for you, be open to the idea that love might show up for you differently this time around. Maybe it's going to grow more slowly. Just because you have a mega spark doesn't mean you're destined to be together, and just because your feelings are more neutral doesn't mean that they won't grow.

Think This:

"I will appreciate what's good about this person, and give myself time to see what develops." Avoid black-and-white thinking here. Say you decide that, on this occasion, you don't want another date. That doesn't mean you're only attracted to emotionally unavailable people. It just means on this occasion, you didn't quite feel enough to continue, and that's okay. It's not a case of there being nice people who you don't connect with, and not-so-nice ones that you do; there are more than two kinds of relationships out there.

Say This:

"Am I looking forward to seeing them again?"

"I want to fall in love with the real person, not my first impression of them."

"I give myself permission to take my time and explore this."

WHAT NEXT?

Successful dating is rarely about a simple yes/no answer. If you've met someone who gives you pause, this could be teaching you something; so don't be afraid to challenge your assumptions about who it is you'll click with.

You Want to Be Honest about Past Relationships

You want to be open about past relationships with the person you're dating because you want them to be fully informed about what they're "signing up for." Honesty is a great start, but make sure that the other person is ready to have that conversation with you, and really listen to what you have to say.

 *Follow these steps to get started:*

1 **Establish some trust before you go full disclosure.**
Think about the timing of your disclosure. Sometimes it's better to be open about things from the get-go. If, for instance, you've got children, it can be smart to make at least a passing reference to this in your dating app profile to filter out anyone who's not open to dating someone with children. However, if you had a difficult breakup or a divorce, you might want to establish that you're interested in dating the other person before sharing this information.

2 **Make it clear that you're over your ex.**
Avoid sharing value judgments about your ex (that they were "crazy," etc.), and instead talk about how what you learned from that relationship has clarified what's important to you in the future.

3 **Remember that everyone has something to disclose.**
Feeling like you've got something you need to tell someone can make you view yourself as being at a disadvantage. What if they don't like what you have to say and reject you? Remind yourself that both of you will have plenty you'll need to open up about; part of what makes a great partner is being able to accept who you are today.

DON'T GO INTO GRANULAR DETAIL RIGHT AWAY. There's detail, and then there's *detail*. It may make you feel better to be totally open about your past, but consider how it might make a new partner feel. They probably don't need to know exactly how many people you slept with before you met, or the grisly details of a breakup. Before you go into the details with someone, make sure they're ready to hear it.

 HERE'S HOW

Always seek the other person's permission to keep sharing. If you're opening up about your past, check in with the other person that they feel comfortable to keep listening. Equally, if someone shuts down conversations when you're trying to emotionally relate to them, take note of this.

Think This:

"What's my intention behind talking about past relationships?" If there's something you feel the other person has a right to hear before proceeding with this relationship, then go ahead. If you want to undermine the other person's feelings of self-worth by talking about how great your ex was, stop right there.

Say This:

"Are you okay with me sharing this with you?"

"Having that relationship taught me a lot about what I really needed in a partner."

"I'm starting to feel like this is becoming a relationship, so I wanted to be open with you about something."

WHAT NEXT? ⟶

As much as conversations like these open you up to the possibility of being rejected by the other person, they also give you the opportunity to be loved and accepted for who you are.

You Thought You Were Going On a Date Together, but They Brought a Friend

You were feeling excited to meet them, the attraction was there, yet suddenly it's turned into a group thing? Maybe your suggestion of a second date has been countered by a suggestion that you join them and their friends doing something, or perhaps their friend just turned up because they "happened to be in the area." You don't want to read too much into this, but isn't gate-crashing kind of rude?

DO THIS *Follow these steps to get started:*

1 Consider whether this could be motivated by safety.
Yes, a date usually is one-on-one, but could the appearance of a friend be because they're concerned about personal safety? If you've invited them to meet at your house, could you swap it up and meet at a public place?

2 Trust your judgment of the situation.
If you think this is in fact because they don't want to commit time to you one-on-one, then think carefully about whether this is something you want to accept. The bare minimum you need from your date to get this show on the road is their willingness to spend time with you.

3 Think about the context before you react.
Are you several dates in and things are going well? If so, this could be your date's not-so-discreet attempt at getting a second opinion from a trusted friend. Is it possible that the friend showing up meant that they were trying to integrate you further into their social life? Or is it really that they're just not that into you?

DON'T ALLOW YOURSELF TO BE DEPRIORITIZED. If you really want to date someone, don't constantly accept being downgraded to "hang out" status. If you over-compromise on the kinds of dates you would like to have just because you really like someone, you won't just lose respect, you'll lose the belief that you deserve better.

 HERE'S HOW

If your date turns up with an unexpected plus-one, don't immediately read this as a negative sign. If their friend really did get locked out of their apartment, or if your date is trying to build a connection with you by inviting their BFF, storming out isn't going to do you any favors. Take a while to figure out the situation, and if it really is the case that you just weren't important enough to them to dedicate time to one-on-one, then make your exit.

Think This:

"I need someone who will give me their time and who (eventually) will make me a priority." Not communicating they're bringing a friend doesn't fully respect your time or your right to a rain check. However, at this early stage of dating, you should still be working out if they could be a good fit for you. If you've found the surprise friend frustrating, or you're not getting enough one-on-one time to build a connection, interpret this as they haven't met your standards, and move on.

Say This:

"I'd like to meet your friends, but can we keep Saturday one-on-one?"

"I'm going to leave you guys to it."

"Of course you can bring a friend to my party."

WHAT NEXT?

Ultimately you need a partner who communicates with you and respects your time. If your dates keep morphing into group hangouts or they make sudden changes to plans and don't consult you, this shouldn't meet your standards. If so, there's no need to be mean about it; just recognize they're not able to give you what you need and move on.

You Like Them in Person, but Their Messages Seem Distant

In the anxiety-ridden world of modern dating, you could be inferring how much someone likes you via how often, and warmly, they message you. How do you keep them interested if it's a while before you can see one another again? And how do you handle it if things are great in person, but you rarely hear from them when you're not together?

 **Follow these steps to get started:**

1 **Remember that keeping your romance alive isn't just on you.**
If there's a big gap between dates, you don't need to mastermind how to keep their interest through messaging. They also must step toward you. If there's a gap of over a week between dates, focus on intermittent yet impactful communication. This means you don't always need to message them "good morning." Instead, keep things fresh by sending them short voice notes, pictures and videos of fun stuff you're doing, etc., every few days. So every time they hear from you, you're sharing something you're genuinely excited about.

2 **Focus on your own needs.**
How easy communication is between you is a good indicator of compatibility. So rather than worrying about the reasons why they're not messaging you as much as you'd like, check in with yourself about whether this interaction is meeting your needs.

3 **Don't jump to the conclusion that they don't like you.**
Some people are less communicative through messaging than others. You might like to message someone throughout the day, but as long as they're consistently setting up real-life dates, give it some time.

DON'T ASSUME THIS IS ALL ABOUT YOU. If it's been a few days and someone hasn't messaged, it can be easy to jump to conclusions ("they led me on!"). However, if you message them with an accusation ("I'm guessing this means you're not interested anymore?"), it won't do you any favors. If you're wrong, you'll come across as insecure, and even if you're right, you'll probably look back on that message in a week's time and cringe.

 HERE'S HOW

If someone's been AWOL, don't start overanalyzing your messages to them, looking for a smoking gun of where you messed things up ("I knew I should have only put one X not two!"). Remember that they have a whole life outside of you, so if you want to check in with them, do it in a non-blaming way (e.g., "Hey, it's been a minute, wanted to see how you are?").

Think This:

"I'm going to stay present and not create a story in my mind as to why they're not messaging me." When you're in the unknown with dating (maybe they haven't messaged in two days!), it can be tempting to stalk a potential date online: This will only make you feel worse. Quit catastrophizing. If you want to talk more, communicate that expectation, and if they still leave you hanging, recognize that this person probably isn't the person who can meet your needs.

Say This:

"I like hearing from you, keep it up ;-)"

"Messages are hard to communicate properly—Face-Time later?"

"Hi, it's been a while. I wanted to see how you are?"

WHAT NEXT?

Before you jump to conclusions, focus on how they're treating you overall. If you're meeting regularly, and they're consistent in other ways, it could be worth giving it a little longer before you delete them from your life.

You Want to Flirt with Someone Online

You know that for someone to see you as a potential date, you have to flirt. But how do you flirt in a way that is cool and sexy, as opposed to cringeworthy and creepy?

 **Follow these steps to get started:**

1 Ask yourself whether you know this person.
What's appropriate flirtation-wise will depend on the context. If you've matched on a dating app (where people are, you know, there to date), then you get more leeway compared to if it's just some hot person you've spotted on social media. Come on too strong to someone who you don't know, and you'll cruise right into the creepy zone. Flirting on social media can be a long shot: Try making a genuine and intelligent comment on one of their posts first, and if this is received well, *then* slide into their DMs.

2 Understand that flirting is a dance that requires reciprocation.
How flirtation works is that you make a small step forward, then see if the other person enthusiastically reciprocates. If they don't, drop it. Without the other person flirting back, you're flirting at them, not with them, and oops: There's that creepy zone again. Try kick-starting your flirtation with a playful comment like, "I don't believe you ;-)" or "You're going to have to convince me ;-)," then see if they play along.

3 Recognize that flirtation can be less about the words you say and more about the tone you use.
For instance, if you want to sound confident and like a leader, keep your words more commanding ("In a meeting, will call later"). If you want to sound coy and inviting, keep your tone softer, like, "Now you've got me curious xx."

DON'T GO TOO SEXUAL TOO SOON. No one needs to see an eggplant emoji popping up in their DMs. Rather than being sexy, being overly sexual before the other person is in the same zone will often come across as socially unaware and turn them off.

 **HERE'S HOW**

If they're giving you nothing to work with, you should lose interest. As a rule of thumb, take your online flirtation only as far as first-date levels of flirting. Many times, people get caught up in flirting outrageously online (going through all the gory details of *exactly* what they're going to do when they meet) then feel too much pressure to ever meet in person. Cool your jets and save your best flirting for the real world.

Think This:	**Say This:**
"Flirting should be fun, light-hearted, and, most importantly, proportional to how well I know this person, and how much they're reciprocating with me."	"I'll make a plan xx."
	"I'm tempted, but will need some convincing…"
	"Surprise me."

WHAT NEXT? ⟶

There's a limit to how much trust, connection, and flirtation you can build virtually. If you're attracted to someone, and the feeling seems mutual, don't ramp up the flirtation too much online. Instead, stay laser focused on how and when you can meet up in the real world.

There's an Awkward Silence on Your Date

It's the date moment everyone dreads: an awkward pause in the conversation. The silence is deafening. You feel like the chance of having a second date is melting away with every second. You search your mind for something to say and end up saying the worst possible thing. How do you stop this conversation from crashing and burning?

 **Follow these steps to get started:**

1 Understand that a pause is only as awkward as you make it.
To end awkward pauses on your dates, you need to stop seeing them as being awkward. A pause in the conversation can in fact be a great time to make eye contact and simmer in some sexual chemistry. If there's a pause in the conversation try to enjoy it.

2 Have a story saved up to share.
If the thought of a pause gives you anxiety, then try having a few go-to stories about your life that you can share on your dates. It can feel counterintuitive to talk about yourself on your dates; however, sharing is an effective way to build trust and help the other person to open up too. Having a couple of stories you've prepared can also help you to feel more confident on your date.

3 Acknowledge what's going on.
A surprisingly confident way to handle awkward silences can be to verbalize what's happening and make a joke out of it. Try saying, "Are we having an awkward silence here? Quick—one of us has got to think of something witty to say!" Said *playfully*, this shows your date that you're socially aware of what's happening and are comfortable in your own skin.

DON'T FEEL LIKE YOU'VE BLOWN IT. Conversations are a two-way process, so it's not all your responsibility to fill the silence. If your inner critic begins to pipe up, telling you that you've ruined things, it will only make it harder for the conversation to organically flow. Take a deep breath and tell yourself that a lull in the conversation is no big deal.

HERE'S HOW

There are clues all around you for where to take the conversation next. Start by thinking about what you'd genuinely like to know about this person. Ask sincere questions. Also listen carefully to their answers: not just what they say, but how they talk about things. Do they seem enthusiastic, unsure, or frustrated talking about a topic? Can you comment on the emotions they're expressing when they speak, as well as the content? The right route forward for the conversation isn't in your head; it's in really listening to what your date is sharing.

Think This:	**Say This:**
"We don't know each other yet, so it's okay for the conversation to take some time to flow. I trust that over time, as we relax, a connection will form if it's supposed to."	Nothing—just make eye contact and smile. "A funny thing happened on my way over to meeting you today…" "There's so much I don't know about you yet. Tell me more about the time when you…"

WHAT NEXT? ⟶

You can bet that there are plenty of people in happy, long-term relationships right now who had a pause or two on their first date. Change how you see an "awkward" silence on your first date; don't give it too much power or meaning. Relax and get back into that conversation.

Chapter 3

GETTING TO KNOW EACH OTHER

You've finally met someone you actually like! Before you announce that you've met "The One" to your friends though, there may well be some anxiety-inducing issues you'll need to address. Modern dating means that just because you're getting along well, doesn't mean that you're necessarily an item. Yup, if you've got the serious feels for someone, then you're going to have to have the "what are we?" talk. This can feel even more complicated if your potential partner is great when you're together but is being inconsistent between your dates. What if you haven't met their friends yet? Or they're always on social media? How do you know where you stand?

This chapter is here to answer these questions and more. Even when you're officially an item, there's some big moments coming up, and this is your guide. Perhaps you know you really want to have kids and are unsure when to bring up that conversation. Maybe you struggle to trust people, and you're worried your fears are going to torpedo another potential relationship. Or what if you've had sex for the first time and it just wasn't that good?! Use this chapter to discover what early relationships are worth working on, and when you should move on.

You Are Having Trouble Being Vulnerable

Surely, to be attractive you need to be cool, confident, and channeling James Bond (or J. Lo) at all times, right? You may think that having a witty one-liner to say is what impresses your dates, but in fact, the ability to be open with someone is a vital relationship-building skill.

 *Follow these steps to get started:*

1 Acknowledge how you're really feeling.
On dates it can be hard to stay present and hold a conversation when you also have a raging internal monologue ("Why did I just say that??"). A way to shush the voices in your head is to verbalize your thoughts. Try telling your dates if you feel nervous, or if you think you've just put your foot in your mouth, or if you dropped some food into your lap. By acknowledging what you're feeling in that moment, you'll stay more present and appear confident.

2 Start small and see how the other person responds.
If the idea of opening up makes your toes curl, start small. Give yourself permission to share your real feelings (just once) and see how the other person responds. Rather than hiding how you feel because you're worried it's going to come out wrong, watch and see if you're pleasantly surprised by the other person's reaction instead.

3 Ask for what you need.
If you're "not good at the relationship thing," a great question to ask yourself is "What do I need to be my best self in this relationship?" For instance, if you find relationships a little claustrophobic, making it clear that you need some personal space during the week to catch up on work can make it easier for you to be tuned in to the relationship the rest of the time.

DON'T PLAY GAMES. If you feel unsure if someone likes you, rather than communicating about how you feel, it can be tempting to play games. They didn't suggest a date this weekend? Well then you're going to take two days to get back to their next message. Playing games deprives you of your chance to be accepted for who you are and doesn't give the other person any guidance as to what you need to be happy.

✔ HERE'S HOW

Multidimensional people are attractive. If you try too hard to be confident, you'll often come across as insecure. Instead, you've got to get used to talking about your feelings. This doesn't have to mean that you treat your dates like a therapy session. But to help people understand you, you need to tell them about your preferences, your doubts, and even your fears. The best people out there for you will enjoy the emotional connection you can share when you open up.

Think This:

"Acceptance is key to forming a healthy relationship." If you don't feel they know you or understand you, how can you expect to feel truly loved? Remember that as much as being shut down can protect you from getting hurt, it can also prevent you from having the experiences you need to heal.

Say This:

"I want to be open with you about something."

"I know not everyone would feel like this, but...is really important to me."

"That was a little awkward. Any chance I can rewind the last three minutes of conversation and start again?"

WHAT NEXT?

You might think that dates require you to be perfect, but they don't. Start experimenting with vulnerability, and see how much further it takes you into your relationships.

You Don't Agree on Values or Politics

They voted for that person?! They're really late all the time, and they think it's okay?! The beauty of meeting new people is that they're not the same as you. When can you learn from the other person, and when is the relationship so incompatible that it's never going to work?

 Follow *these steps* *to get started:*

1 **Understand you need only *some* things in common for this to work.**
As a start point, know that a great relationship isn't like a game of Snap: You don't need to like all the same things. Yes, it can make life easier if you have a shared love of doubles Ping-Pong or swing dance, but interests like these are "nice to haves" rather than essential relationship building blocks. Get away from needing to share the same hobbies as your dates. Compatible doesn't mean "the same." Let it go if they don't like the same sports as you, and spend more time working out if your values line up.

2 **Practice tolerance.**
Here's the deal: There is no perfect person for you. Everyone will have something that you find slightly tedious. Maybe they're a stickler for punctuality. Or they read a lot of conspiracy theories on the Internet. Don't try to search for a perfect person: Decide whether being with this person is worth the trade-off that they can be a little annoying sometimes.

3 **Take time to hear them out, and don't immediately judge them.**
A difference of opinion can rapidly escalate into an all-out meltdown when neither side takes time to listen to the other one. If you really want to annoy someone, cut them off midsentence, turn the conversation back to yourself, and make a damning judgment like, "I could never be with someone who..." If you want to get better at relationships, listen.

DON'T HAVE TOO-RIGID STANDARDS AROUND WHO YOU DATE. Whether it's the people you select for dates in the first place, or bailing out in the early stages of dating because someone doesn't have *exactly* the same views as you, having standards in the wrong places can seriously obstruct you in your quest to find love. Start to question if this big list of wants is really serving you, or whether you could do with practicing some more flexibility with your type.

 ## HERE'S HOW

Question how fundamental each value is to you. Not all values are made equal. If, for example, one of you wants to spend every day together and sees themself having a family one day, while the other loves their independence and doesn't want kids, that could be a really big gap to cross. If they're naturally more social, while you like time one-on-one, this could be easier to negotiate. Is something fundamentally important to you, or just a preference?

Think This:

"Can I accept them, even if I don't understand them?" You will not always fully understand your partner. Instead of needing to understand all their motivations, can you take a step back and ask yourself if you can just accept them for who they are instead? Or not?

Say This:

"I'm not here to judge you; I want to understand."

"I don't fully understand yet, but I really accept that's important to you."

"I like you a lot as a person, but for me, not wanting children is a deal-breaker."

WHAT NEXT?

Actively challenge your assumptions about what you need in a relationship. If you find communication easy, you share common life goals, and you feel great in their company, then you might want to overlook a smaller mismatch.

You Have Your First Fight

You feel disoriented, your heart is beating more loudly, and you've quite possibly turned off your cell phone in annoyance. You've had your first fight, and realized your partner isn't a faultless super-person. However, you now have the opportunity to take your relationship to the next level, wrapped in the unexpected packaging of your first fight.

 *Follow these steps to get started:*

1 Give it some time.
No one is their best self late at night, after alcohol has been drunk, or during a long car journey. Before you write off this relationship, give both of you some leeway for context. Were you tired? Was it late? Were nerves frayed? In the heat of the moment, people rarely act in the best interests of the relationship. An argument that feels like the end of the world one day, might be cleared up the next.

2 Listen to them.
If you constantly walk away at the first sign of trouble you deprive yourself not only of the opportunity to get to know them better, but also to understand yourself better. Listen to them in a way you've never bothered to listen to someone before.

3 Recognize that you can either be right or you can be happy.
Don't operate from the space of needing someone to always agree with everything you say (isn't that called a dictatorship?). Instead, accept that it's okay to be in the wrong or to just have a difference of opinion. Neither of these will break a relationship; needing to be right and "win" the argument will.

DON'T PANIC AND CATASTROPHIZE; IT'S (PROBABLY) NOT ALL OVER. When you have an argument, you may flip into panic mode. This beautiful, cozy relationship you've established feels like it's burning to the ground around you. You're disoriented: Will you need to go on dating apps again? Should you send them one last message to let them know how you *really* feel? All relationships experience conflict. It's not about the fact that you've had a fight; it's how you resolve it that counts.

✔ HERE'S HOW

High up on your checklist of what you really need in a partner should be the ability to come back to the table after a fallout. If, after a quarrel, they emotionally withdraw to glacial levels, "spread their risk" by setting up a date with someone else, or hold a major grudge, consider getting out. If they can say sorry (yes, you have to say it too), take the time to listen to you, and don't see this as spelling the end of your relationship, you could have a keeper here.

Think This:

"In the long run, I'm aiming for harmony in this relationship." If you generally feel stable, secure, and happy with this person, a few arguments here and there are just normal! File it under "no big deal" in your mind. However, if your relationship is more on and off than a light switch, then this isn't exciting or passionate; it's unhealthy.

Say This:

"I didn't like fighting with you yesterday, and I'm sorry for my part in it."

"I think I jumped to some conclusions yesterday, and I'd really like the chance to understand you better."

"I'm feeling hurt, but I'd like to hug it out."

WHAT NEXT?

A first fight isn't the end. It's a milestone in your relationship. Honestly, it is almost a cause for celebration: You've reached a new level of emotional intimacy! Now focus on the bigger picture of how well you both resolve this temporary stumbling block.

You Don't Like Their Friends, and Their Friends Don't Like You

Meeting friends is a big relationship milestone...but what if you don't like each other? Will they sabotage the relationship? Or are you going to have to tolerate spending time with people you don't like? Can you really make up excuses not to go to that many of their birthdays?

 Follow these steps to get started:

1 Attempt to get to know people one-on-one.
Group settings can bring out the worst in people. People are usually better one-on-one. Meeting this way will make it easier for you to both empathize with one another, and people will (usually) be more authentic. Try to divide and conquer by setting up opportunities to get to know their friends in a setting that doesn't exacerbate their pack instincts.

2 Accept that these people are here to stay, so now it's time for you to work on those relationships.
For the most part, their friends will be here to stay. So don't waste too much time conjuring up Machiavellian ways of breaking apart those relationships. This isn't a Shakespeare play or reality TV; you're probably going to know these people for a very long time. Start with this assumption, and work to build the best relationships you can with them.

3 Give your partner freedom to spend time with their friends, even if you take a back seat.
Getting between your partner and their friends presents yourself as insecure and controlling. Stop your partner's normal routine of poker nights, tennis matches, or nights out, and you'll probably make them think long and hard about whether the trade-off of being with you is worth it.

DON'T FAN THE FLAMES OF CONFLICT. Even if you think your partner's friends are total idiots, don't tell them this. Criticizing their friends puts your partner in a difficult position of having to choose between you. It also makes you look bad. If you really can't stand them, at least strive for neutrality in how you talk about them: It makes it much harder for them to have an issue with you if you're always taking the higher ground.

HERE'S HOW

So you didn't hit it off. Worse things have happened. Start to open your mind to the possibility that one day you *might* like them, even if you're never super close. To get you to this place, say yes to group invites, and encourage your partner to catch up with them individually too. See your relationship with them as one that is a bit of a fixer-upper, but isn't a total write-off.

Think This:

"Not liking one another doesn't have to last forever." Even the rockiest of relationships can settle down over time into mutual understanding and acceptance—if given the opportunity. You don't need an immediate connection to make this work. You need both sides to make an effort to get to know one another.

Say This:

"You should go catch up with them. I'm really happy just chilling tonight."

"Okay, that sounds great. I'd love to go to their party."

"I feel like I haven't had the chance to click with [friend] yet. Perhaps we could invite them over for dinner?"

WHAT NEXT? —————————————————→

Your mission from here on out is to be the bigger person. If you don't rise to any snide remarks, and if you channel being relaxed, neutral, and open-minded, you're going to be a hard person to dislike.

You Are Scared to Meet Their Family

But why? You're so awesome! Okay, maybe you know that part, but the thought of their nearest and dearest passing judgment on you can still feel scary. Stop seeing this is an opportunity for failure, and start seeing it as an opportunity to grow closer to your partner.

 **Follow these steps to get started:**

1 Make an effort.
Simple things like being on time, brushing your hair, and bringing a gift can do a lot to make a good first impression. Even if you're a little "different," trust that most people will have the emotional intelligence to realize when two people are good for one another.

2 Ask questions and be interested in them.
You may not fully get their dad's obsession with sports, or quite share their mom's enthusiasm for country walks, but joining in will get you a long way. If you coo over family albums, and spring out of bed to join them on their annual 10K run, then they will recognize your effort as an indication of how much you care about your relationship.

3 Give way to family time.
Okay, so the idea of a board game night might bore you, but it's important here to participate in family time. If they sense their child is becoming more distant since they met you, then this will ruffle feathers.

DON'T PUT THEM ON A PEDESTAL. Even if their parents are really clever, rich, good-looking, or champion lacrosse players, this doesn't mean that they won't like you. Most well-balanced, grown-up people aren't fixated on achievement, so don't feel like you're coming up short next to them.

 HERE'S HOW

Developing a relationship with your partner's family is a marathon, not a sprint, so not everything is going to hinge on this first meeting with them. Choose a relaxed first meeting if you can, and focus on the positive sign here that your partner is excited to bring you further into their life. First meetings can be awkward, so don't think it's a bust if you don't have immediate chemistry with their parents.

Think This:

"I'm building a relationship not just with my partner, but with their whole family." At the start of a relationship, you might feel there's a conflict between time spent together as a couple and your partner's family commitments. Yes, it can be annoying to cancel your date night for a baby shower, but this doesn't just go one way. If your partner is close to their family, chances are they'll make an effort with your family too. Families can be demanding, but a great relationship with your in-laws can also be incredibly rewarding.

Say This:

"I know it's a long way, but it's your brother, so we should really make an effort to go."

"I'm really looking forward to it. Is there anything you'd like me to bring?"

"I'm so lucky to have met..."

WHAT NEXT?

A few compromises at the start of getting to know your partner's family can really set you up for the future. Imagine if you know these people for the next five years, ten years, maybe forever? Recognize the opportunity here to form new relationships that will help to support you and your partner. They don't call them your mother- and father-in-law for nothing.

You're Not Sure How Upfront You Should Be about Wanting (or Not Wanting) Kids

Maybe you've always known you don't want kids and are worried you will burst your partner's bubble when they find out diapers don't feature in your life plan. Or maybe your biological clock is more Big Ben than wristwatch; having a family is a major life goal of yours. So you need to bring up the kids thing ASAP, but how? Could it put them off? Will they run for the hills if they think you're only interested in them for their sperm or their ovaries?

 Follow these steps to get started:

1 **Suggest your interest in children from the get-go.**
A well-placed photo of you playing with your nephews on your dating app profile helps to communicate your family values. You can also take a moment to notice how engaged they are with you when you mention your love of the little people in your life.

2 **Make it about your life goals, not about them.**
Instead of asking, "Do you want kids?" you can start the conversation more smoothly by saying, "If I meet the right person, I'd love children one day" or "I've always known having children just wasn't for me."

3 **Keep your focus on meeting the right person.**
No one wants to meet someone and immediately be sized up for their parental potential, or jump right into talking about where you'll be in fifty years. People want you to choose them because of how you connect, not just because they neatly fit into your life plan.

DON'T BRING UP THE KIDS QUESTION IN YOUR FIRST MESSAGES TO SOMEONE. Asking someone if they want kids (or not) doesn't usually make for great chat on a dating app. Spend at least a few dates establishing you have compatibility before asking them about their wider life goals.

HERE'S HOW

A great way to kick-start this tricky conversation can be by expressing what you want. In a conversation people usually reciprocate with the same level of information. So if you say that you love children and they respond with tumbleweeds, this probably isn't a great sign. If asking, "So do you see yourself having kids?" also feels too direct, try asking them about their bucket list. Then listen. Does their five-year plan involve traveling through Latin America? Or finding someone to start a family with?

Think This:

"I need to focus on the connection I'm experiencing with them first, and then establish if we have the same long-term goals." The kids thing can be incredibly stressful. As if dating wasn't hard enough, it's worse if you feel you have a ticking time bomb in the background. Yes, you have to be realistic about time (unfortunately fertility doesn't last forever) but don't let time bully you. If you're in a hurry to make a decision about someone, chances are you might make the wrong one.

Say This:

"I'm actually such a family person, I'd love kids of my own one day."

"So what's on your bucket list?"

"I've always known that I didn't want children. For me, career, travel, and forming a great partnership have always been my priorities."

WHAT NEXT? ⟶

If the conversation about kids is causing you anxiety, you may just want to bring it up. Remember: The best partners for you are going to be on a similar page. Yes, there's a chance they won't be open to the same things, but there's an equal chance that they will be.

You Need to Have the "What Are We?" Talk

Finally you've met someone you're excited about. There's only one snag though: You have no idea where you stand. It feels like a relationship, but because you haven't had "the talk," how do you know where you stand?

 **Follow these steps to get started:**

1 Consider whether the timing is right for this conversation.
Commitment is a pretty big deal: You want to feel confident that you've formed a genuine connection before you go exclusive. Don't commit to first impressions; commit to how they show up for you in the longer run.

2 Communicate.
You may feel awkward about being the initiator of this conversation (if they liked you enough, surely they would bring it up...right?). Rather than fretting about who goes first, sometimes it's more valuable to you to get clear on where you stand. Remember that there's nothing wrong with saying something; if you're being intimate (both physically and emotionally), it would be weird not to.

3 Start with what you want.
Saying, "What is this?" can feel like a bombshell. It will feel more natural to express your own feelings. That could be around sexual exclusivity ("I like to focus on one person at a time") or exclusivity in general ("At this point, it would feel strange for me to be seeing other people").

DON'T ASSUME THE STATUS OF YOUR RELATIONSHIP. One of the tricky bits about modern dating is that you can be messaging someone every day, be physically intimate, and still not be in an official relationship. So don't assume that just because you have an amazing connection and you're doing relationship things, that you're there yet.

 HERE'S HOW

Kick-start the conversation: Remember that this isn't about getting a yes from them. Even if you discover they don't want the same things as you, while this is disappointing in the moment, their answer will give you clarity in the longer run. If you're clear that you want commitment, then you need to check out if this person is on the same page as you or not. Then you need to listen to them: If they say they really like you, *but*...don't kid yourself that they'll change their mind. Likewise, if they dodge the subject altogether, then this is telling you something too.

Think This:

"Ultimately I want to be in a loving, committed relationship. If the person I'm dating isn't aligned with this, I need to find someone who is." Your end goal is more important than your connection to them. Yes, it's tough when you really like someone, but don't convince yourself that you're happy with a no-strings-attached relationship just so you can keep them in your life. You shouldn't need to arm-twist anyone into committing to you.

Say This:

"I wanted to be open that this is starting to feel like a relationship to me."

"Just so you know, I've deleted my dating apps."

"I want to concentrate on you and see where this could go, but I didn't want to assume anything, so thought I should check in with you first."

WHAT NEXT?

You've had "the talk," you've listened to what they had to say, and now it's time to act on it. If they don't want commitment, it's probably more about what stage they're at in their life than it is about you. Accept that this is where they stand, and if it doesn't line up with what you want, let it go.

Your Partner Is Being Controlling

It was all going so well. Then they shushed you that time in the taxi when they thought you were talking too loudly. They scrunched up their face in disapproval when you showed them the outfit you wanted to wear. Is there a darker side to your relationship? Are you beginning to find your partner controlling?

 *Follow these steps to get started:*

1 Consider whether this is a clash over how much independence and/or control you both want.
People can sometimes have mismatched needs for independence in a relationship: One person expects to spend every weekend together; the other likes to have more flexibility to catch up with friends. Mismatched levels of intimacy are one relationship problem; a controlling partner is another. Do they micromanage you? Are they jealous? Do they try to limit your contact with friends and family? Then this could be control.

2 Keep an incident log.
Yes, it sounds like something that your HR department has, but it can be hard to put your finger on controlling behavior. When someone's loving one minute and critical the next, it's emotionally confusing. Keep a private note-to-self about things they say and do that don't feel right to you.

3 Be open with friends and family about what you're going through.
A controlling partner may try to keep you distant from friends and family, from sulking if you go out with friends (to let you know that if you do that again, you'll have to deal with their bad mood) to outright telling you that your friends are no good for you. Trust the social relationships that you've had for a long time, and be open with them about your relationship.

DON'T CONSTANTLY GIVE IN TO THEM TO AVOID AN ARGUMENT. The thing about boundaries is they only work if you stick to them. If you say you're going to leave but don't, it will become an empty threat. If seeing your friends, having a second slice of cake, or wearing that outfit is important to you, do it.

 HERE'S HOW

Controlling behavior often starts subtly, so if you're unsure whether to stay or go, try to communicate. If your attempts to talk are ignored, or promises are made then broken, perhaps this is the final signal you need to get out.

Think This:

"I need to return to myself and get some headspace to see this situation clearly." If you gave up a hobby to spend more time with your partner, pick it back up. Book in time with your friends. Research new places you could move to. Devote some mental energy to imagining what a future could be like without them in it.

Say This:

"I don't feel supported when you give me feedback like that. It's really important to me that I feel heard."

"When you say that you don't want me to see my friends, I feel trapped. I want to understand why that's so important to you."

"I'm going out now, as I don't want to let my friends down. I'll message you when I'm on my way home."

WHAT NEXT? ⟶

Don't be afraid to walk away. And if you are afraid to walk away, seek support to help you to get out. Controlling and abusive behavior often escalates at the end of a relationship. If you fear this might be the case, contact a domestic abuse support service (as well as friends and family), which can give you step-by-step support to leave your relationship safely.

You Are Struggling to Trust Your Partner

You love your partner, but you're starting to feel like you can't trust them. If alarm bells are ringing about your partner's fidelity, how do you separate out your insecurities from when you really need to question their behavior?

 **Follow these steps to get started:**

1 Ask yourself whether this is about them or about you.
Has trust been an issue in previous relationships? If so, distinguish between what's arising in the here-and-now that's triggering your feelings of distrust, and what from the past is meddling with your happiness today. A licensed therapist or counselor can help you to process your feelings.

2 Ask for reassurance.
If you're feeling insecure, it will take courage to open up, but someone who's a good partner for you will be able to give you the stability you need to calm your anxieties. Don't keep your feelings to yourself. If it's not the right time to talk to your partner, share how you're feeling with a supportive friend.

3 If you notice a red flag, verbalize it.
There's a chance here that your gut instinct might be right. However, rather than having a conspiracy theory about your own relationship, you need to talk to your partner about what you've noticed and check out their reaction. Did you stumble across a flirtatious online chat? Do they still have a dating app on their phone? Don't sit on information like this; take a deep breath and ask them about it.

DON'T CREATE A STORY IN YOUR MIND ABOUT WHAT'S GOING ON THAT MAY NOT BE TRUE. If you don't communicate with your partner about how you are feeling, your insecurities may fester. Soon every time they go online or stay late at work might act like a hair trigger for you—but you won't be reacting to what they're actually doing. You'll be reacting to the story you've told yourself about what their behavior means. Don't create a work of fiction in your head about your relationship; talk to your partner.

HERE'S HOW

Ultimately, you need a partner who is able to give you the stability you need to thrive. Yes, you may need to work on your trust issues, but you also need to be with someone who is transparent and inclusive enough to help you to feel secure. Look for partners who are open books, where communication is easy, and where you want similar levels of closeness. Becoming more trusting may start small for you: not checking their social media, or being okay with them having a night out with friends.

Think This:

"Giving trust is a necessary step to having the relationship I want." Yes, giving trust involves a leap of faith, but you could also experience how secure you will feel knowing you can give someone freedom, and that freedom will never be abused. Assume your partner has good intentions, and gradually open up.

Say This:

"I want to check something out with you that's been playing on my mind."

"I've been feeling worried about [behavior]. I need some reassurance."

"I trust you."

WHAT NEXT? ⟶

Trust (or distrust) compounds. It would be unrealistic to trust someone you've just met overnight, but if your partner has consistently behaved in a loving and trustworthy way, keep taking those leaps of faith. Everyone has had disappointments when people have let them down, but just because it happened one time doesn't mean it will happen every time.

You're Spending the Night with Your Partner for the First Time

Hang on, let's put Barry White on...this is exciting! You're about to take your relationship to the next level. You're excited, but also a bit nervous. Will you have chemistry? Will it be awkward? Will they still like you after you've made that level of physical commitment?

 *Follow these steps to get started:*

1 Take this at your own pace.
There's no rush to "go there" (and if there is, that's not a great sign about your partner). In fact, there are loads of ways you can be intimate without going the whole way: kissing, naked cuddles, and foreplay can all help you to relax and get used to a new partner. Rushed intimacy is often bad intimacy.

2 Laugh about it.
Intimacy is erotic, sensual, and quite frequently funny. If a body part isn't playing ball, or something isn't quite working, laugh about it. It happens to everyone. Get away from the need for your first time together to be perfect; it's an experiment. If you can laugh about it, you'll help your partner to relax too.

3 Give yourselves time to get to know what works.
It's highly unlikely that the first time you are intimate will be the best time. So don't think that every time will be the same. If things don't quite click, focus on communicating your preferences to them.

DON'T WORRY YOU'RE NOT DOING IT "RIGHT." Intimacy isn't about doing an obscure position from the Kama Sutra; it's about being present, communicating, and connecting with your partner. Do a Tantra course, or speak to a sex coach, and build a better sexual relationship with yourself, not just your partner.

 HERE'S HOW

Your goal tonight is to be present and communicate with your partner. Turn your phone off, spend time relaxing with them, and consistently ask (and check in with yourself too) before taking the next step. You're not looking for an "Er, sure…"; you're looking for enthusiastic consent from your partner. If there's hesitancy on either part, just stop and dial it back a few steps. Be open about what you need to feel turned on and how you like things to be done.

Think This:

"It is a big deal, but it's also not a big deal." Yes, being intimate for the first time does mark a new milestone in your relationship. However, if you stick with this person over the long run, you're going to experience all different kinds of intimacy. So-good-it's-an-out-of-body-experience sex, tired sex, lazy sex, bad sex, because-we-think-we-should sex, and every intimate activity in between. So it won't always be like this.

Say This:

"I want to take the next step, if you're ready too?"

"I actually really like it when…"

"I like you, but I need more time. Can we stick to kissing for now?"

WHAT NEXT?

Give yourselves time to grow into this part of your relationship. Yes, you might be rushing home from your first night together messaging all your friends with the mind-blowing details. However, if it wasn't what you expected, don't feel like the whole relationship is a write-off. Do you have a partner that is willing to learn? Can you be a good teacher? If everything else about the relationship is working for you, be open to trying.

You Aren't Happy with Your Sexual Relationship

Life's too short to have bad sex! So you're stuck: Do you go back to the drawing board and try to meet someone else? Or do you accept that you may never be sexually satisfied? Luckily, these aren't your only options.

 Follow these steps to get started:

1 Consider whether you can rewind your relationship ten steps.
Can you take the pressure off your sex life by focusing on all the steps that lead up to sex, rather than sex itself? Instead of withdrawing because your sexual needs aren't being met, can you up the affection toward your partner? Kissing, cuddling, and spending quality time together (naked or not) will help to remind you of your physical connection.

2 Determine (honestly) whether you have really communicated what you need.
Have you been passive-aggressive? Have you sulked when you're not sexually satisfied? Or have you been able to openly, and in a non-blaming way, instruct your partner as to what good sex looks like to you? By getting real about how you feel about your sex life, you might just give yourselves the opportunity to start to reconnect.

3 Ask whether you can feel more sexual within yourself.
Is there a way that you can reconnect to your own sexual desire? Everything from kundalini yoga, to massage, to erotic films and books, or just writing down your own fantasies, can help you feel more sexually switched on. Your partner doesn't create the spark in you; you create it within yourself.

DON'T MAKE YOUR PARTNER FEEL BAD. When your sex life isn't satisfying it can feel emotionally bruising. You may want to withdraw or be critical because your needs aren't getting met. However, for your partner to stand the best chance of being able to meet your needs, they need to feel like they can win. Instead of sniping at them, how can you build their confidence?

 **HERE'S HOW**

What *is* working? Do you like kissing your partner? Is there a kind of foreplay that you love? Is there a course you could take together to educate yourselves more about sex? Instead of letting this issue divide you, can you rise to the challenge to tackle this as a team?

<table>
<tr><td>

Think This:

"What's the story I keep telling myself about my sex life?" Is your sex life terrible? Is your partner a bad lover? Or have you just hit a dry spell because of external pressures in your life? The narrative you create around your problems can become bigger than the problem itself. Is there a way you can see this as less of a big deal? Less make or break, and more something to work on?

</td><td>

Say This:

"We're always tired mid-week so let's save Saturday afternoons just for us."

"I really enjoy kissing you; let's do more of that."

"I found this course that I think could be fun for us to take together."

</td></tr>
</table>

WHAT NEXT? ⟶

It's normal to go through different phases with your sex life: from the orgasmic to the bland. Just because you're in a bland phase right now doesn't mean you can't get back to an orgasmic one; and nearly every relationship you have (no matter how great the sex is at the start) will face similar challenges at some point. If you feel you've exhausted all your options, and things still are just not working out in the bedroom, then the last step you can take is to accept that you have a wonderful friendship but that you need to have passion for it to be a relationship.

You Don't Have Any Hobbies in Common

The more you've gotten to know your partner, you're starting to realize that you don't have much in common. You like to get out and about, and they like "just chilling." You prefer spending time one-on-one, and they're a real extrovert. Can you reach a happy middle ground, or are you just not that compatible?

 Follow these steps to get started:

1 **Consider whether you can introduce your partner to your hobbies.**
Maybe you've already tried this, but can you try again? Trying something new can feel daunting. Could any reluctance from your partner be shyness or insecurity? Is there a way you can make your hobby more approachable? If you love hiking for example, can you start with an easy trail? Get them some new hiking boots? Or promise they can DJ the whole car ride home?

2 **Try showing more interest in what they like.**
Participate in their world, and they'll be more willing to participate in yours. Even if they like solo activities like reading, can you snuggle up next to them on the sofa as they do it?

3 **Ask whether you can balance time between both your needs.**
There are enough hours in the day for you to both be able to get your needs met. Your gold standard for whether you can work through your differences should be about whether you're both willing to compromise. If they're flexible in trying out your hobbies (and you theirs), their willingness to improve the relationship is more valuable than having everything in common.

DON'T BELIEVE YOU NEED TO HAVE EVERYTHING IN COMMON TO MAKE YOUR RELATIONSHIP WORK. You don't need a partner who is entirely the same as you; you need a partner who is compatible. And these are two different things. There are plenty of work-arounds for a difference in hobbies: You can spend time apart, you can compromise, or you can even have a rotation of whose hobby you focus on each day or week.

 HERE'S HOW

Don't let a difference in hobbies blight your weekend or become a constant source of tension. If your partner believes your hobby is encroaching on your quality time together, seek a compromise: Invite them along, schedule quality time together, and help them to understand why it's important for you to do this.

Think This:

"Is my partner sharing this hobby essential to our relationship happiness?" Yes, it might be nice to have a partner who loves the same sports as you. Just think about that; there would never be any battles over the remote! However, if your partner is happy for you to keep up your hobbies, is there a real issue with having this time apart? You can't get absolutely everything in one person (and if you think you can, be prepared to stand corrected).

Say This:

"I'd love you to come along, even if it's just for half an hour."

"There's a good spa next to the gym where you could go while I work out?"

"What would you like to do this weekend?"

WHAT NEXT? ⟶

On the scale of relationship problems this one has some of the easier fixes. As long as both partners are willing to compromise, then enjoying doing different things shouldn't be an issue in the long run. If it is, or they're not willing to compromise, then the issue isn't about not having enough in common. It's about not having a partnership with enough flexibility and communication for everyone to get their needs met.

Your Pet Doesn't Like Them

You really like your partner, but a very special person in your life doesn't. Okay...they're not a person, but you love them like your own child. Your pet hates your partner. This is more common than you'd think. Pets can be territorial or have a hard time sharing the people they love, especially if they come from a tough background. You don't want to end your relationship, but you need to help your fur baby accept there's a new person in your life. How?

 Follow these steps to get started:

1 **Consider offering your pet treats when your partner is around.**
Yes, it's a little like bribery, but you want your pet to associate positive things with your new partner rather than being aggrieved that they've taken their spot in your bed.

2 **Encourage your partner to remain calm and neutral around your pet.**
This can be tricky when your pet is making an all-out assault: loud noises, pooping in their shoes, and tearing your furniture to shreds. Help your partner to understand this isn't how they normally behave, and that they should remain patient so your pet can eventually figure out that this new person isn't a threat.

3 **Consider whether there is anything you can do to make your partner appear less threatening.**
Heavy boots, big coats, hands in pockets, and sometimes even facial hair can all spook animals. Is there a simple styling change your partner can make to appear more pet-friendly?

DON'T FORCE YOUR PARTNER AND YOUR PET TOGETHER; ALLOW YOUR PET TO COME TO THEM IN THEIR OWN TIME. Don't try and put your pet on your partner's lap, and if you're going out of town, choose someone your pet knows better to come around to feed them.

 HERE'S HOW

See these coming weeks (maybe more) as an adjustment period. Your pet will need time to accept your new partner, so don't rush the process. If your pet is particularly anxious, it may also be smart for your new partner to stay at your house more, so that they're not left home alone for long periods of time. Animals can adapt, but it can be harder for them if they've experienced abuse in the past.

Think This:	**Say This:**
"This adjustment period may be challenging, but it will end." This is absolutely not a deal-breaker—provided you are confident that your partner isn't behaving in an abusive way toward your pet. This is going to be a tricky period, but there's every chance for acceptance from your pet on the other side.	"Would you be able to come over to my place? Frou-Frou gets a little anxious if I'm out for a long time." "Here, offer him this treat. He loves anyone who feeds him." "I wouldn't put your shoes on ground level until Fido settles down."

WHAT NEXT?

If you love animals, you need a partner who at least happily tolerates them. Perhaps one day you dream of having a huge pet family, so make sure you're on (roughly) the same page if this is the case. If your partner has an allergy that makes hanging out with your pet off-putting, for the short term you can stay at their house more, and in the longer run you could swap out soft furnishings for hard surfaces. There's plenty of compromises on the table here, so give it time, and you could still be one happy, furry family.

You're Planning Your First Vacation Together

A holiday together is another one of those lovely early relationship milestones: no kids, no commitments, just good wine and a comfy hotel bed, perfect. However, like most things you love, vacations can also be stressful. Just as you're settling into a sun lounger, you can be hit with an unexpected test of your compatibility as a couple.

 Follow these steps to get started:

1 Compromise on your itinerary.
One of you may like to plan every second of your holidays, while the other would rather lounge in the spa. Be conscious not to overplan your time together, and allow downtime to be spontaneous. You may also find that you have different ideas about how much time you want to spend together; if this is the case, don't be afraid to spend time apart. A holiday isn't a contract to spend every waking second doing exactly the same thing.

2 Stay present.
Don't spend your vacation checking your work email or capturing every moment for social media. One of the best things you can do to really connect with your partner is to get offline and have some lo-fi time. Consider packing a board game or a deck of cards, and get to know one another the old-school way.

3 Agree on a budget.
No one likes to talk about money, but a way to ruin a holiday is for one partner to spend more than they're comfortable with. Go on a vacation that works financially for the partner that has the lower income, or, if you're the higher earner, step in to pay more.

DON'T EVEN GO THERE WITH THAT DEEP AND MEANING-FUL TALK; THIS IS A TRIED-AND-TESTED WAY TO RUIN A HOLIDAY. For some strange reason, late at night, one bottle of wine down, on a vacation may feel like a great time to get something off your chest, but it really isn't. If you fall out, you're both miles from home, stuck in a hotel room together. This is a recipe for disaster. Save the big talk for when you're back home, and keep your holiday focused on creating fun memories together.

 HERE'S HOW

Just like you wouldn't go for a three-course meal for a first date, don't go on a two-week vacation as your first holiday together. Remember that as magical as this time will be, it is also a test of your compatibility, so dip your toe in the water with a minibreak first.

Think This:

"I will keep my expectations realistic and not feel disappointed if everything's not perfect." High expectations often lead to serious disappointments. Undoubtedly in the run-up to your vacation your mind may wander to how amazing it's going to be: the food, the free time, the intimacy.…Fast-forward a few weeks when your bags have gotten lost at the airport, and this perfect image you had in your head will unravel. So try to balance any fantasizing you do with practical steps like budgeting and sharing an itinerary.

Say This:

"That place looks amazing, but is a little beyond my budget—could we try this one instead?"

"Maybe we shouldn't plan anything for the first few days so we can see how we feel when we get there."

"Okay, my phone's off. Shall we go for Uno or strip poker?"

WHAT NEXT? ⟶

Your vacation is probably going to be fantastic. But if, for whatever reason, it isn't, remember that this is also about compatibility. Can you laugh about it when your flight is delayed? Not feel like something's wrong if you don't have sex? Can you rise to challenges as a team?

Your Partner Is Addicted to Social Media

Call you old-fashioned, but you just don't get social media. Having to take a dozen photos of them on your date nights is getting tedious. The fact that they haven't once mentioned you on their profile seems odd. And what about those followers they seem so familiar with? How do you handle it when your partner's addicted to social media?

 **Follow these steps to get started:**

1 **Understand their reasons for being on social media so much.**
If you're not a social media user, being around someone who constantly takes a *lot* of selfies can feel bewildering. However, don't jump to the conclusion that they're doing this because they're vain. Be open-minded and get to know their reasons for being online so much. Do they see it as essential to their career? Is it how they stay in touch with friends?

2 **Ask why they don't want to say they're in a relationship.**
If they don't mention you on social media, stop short of jumping to conclusions. If they have an account that's professional, it may be incongruous to drop in a mention of their date. Perhaps they're a private person outside of their social media life. Don't assume that appearing single online is all about having the license to cheat.

3 **Understand that their online life is separate from their real one.**
Social media isn't real life. So before you get too annoyed at how they're using social media, consider first how things are going in the real world. Have they introduced you to friends and family? If they're including you in their life in the real world, this is usually more meaningful than writing a post about you.

DON'T ASSUME THAT EVERY FOLLOWER THEY HAVE IS A POTENTIAL DATE. It may make you sick to your stomach to see that they follow a lot of celebrity accounts online. Or it may bug you that that one person always posts a love heart emoji in response to every photo they post, but this doesn't mean they're being unfaithful. Chances are they've put very little thought into who they follow. Try to park this as an insecurity, not a threat to your relationship.

 HERE'S HOW

They love social media; you barely use it. You may initially feel like there's a mismatch here, but over time you may find equilibrium. People may use social media more when they're single: They have more free time, they get validation from their fans, and it can be a tool to get dates too. However, as they become more content in your relationship, their online life may lose some of its sparkle. And even if it doesn't, perhaps you can grow to understand their use of social media more, so it no longer feels like a threat.

Think This:	**Say This:**
"Is everything else about this relationship working for me?" Don't jump to conclusions; think about how happy you are in the relationship holistically.	"Okay, give me some direction here and I'll get a good photo of you."
	"I know updating your profile's important to you but I want us both to be present for this."
	"I know social media is a much bigger part of your life than mine, and I want to understand why it's important for you."

WHAT NEXT? ⟶

Like most parts of compatibility, a mismatch in social media consumption doesn't have to make or break a connection. Provided your real-world relationship is strong, one person's social media addiction doesn't have to be a red flag for your relationship.

They Want to Take Things *Really* Slowly

This time you want to get it right—and you're okay to take things slowly, just not *this* slowly. Maybe you haven't met their friends or family yet, maybe your physical connection has stalled at kissing, or maybe you're still trying to get them to meet you in the first place. Should you be respectful of their pace? Or is this tortoise of a relationship a nonstarter that you need to walk away from?

 Follow these steps to get started:

1 Consider whether you've actually met yet.
If they're taking things so slowly that you haven't gone on an actual date yet, this is a red flag. Be wary of entering into a long messaging exchange over weeks with someone who can't meet you in person, or at least hop on a video call. At best, this could be someone who can't commit their time to building a relationship; at worst, they might not be who they say they are.

2 Clue into their communication.
If someone has a preference to take things slowly, have they been open with you about their preferences, and reassured you that they're interested? Or are your attempts to get closer to them being met with a barrage of excuses as to why that can't happen?

3 Recognize any feelings of exclusion.
Did they throw a party and leave you off the guest list? Were they aloof about their Valentine's Day plans? Have they not followed you on social media? Be cautious if you feel siloed from the rest of their life; this could mean that they're less interested in taking things slowly, and more preoccupied with keeping their options open.

DON'T DISREGARD YOUR OWN NEEDS FOR INTIMACY. It's normal for you to want to spend time with someone you like, and to express physical affection. Provided you don't expect all of this to happen overnight, try not to overthink your own needs for physical and emotional intimacy. It can be valuable to take your time getting to know someone, but you also shouldn't feel constantly frustrated or confused by the pace of the relationship.

HERE'S HOW

Everyone has different preferences for how much intimacy they like. Some people want to jump in with both feet and enjoy the excitement of a new romance, while other people like to build a friendship first. Ideally you want to date someone who is in roughly the same ballpark as you in terms of how they like to get to know someone. You also want to be switched on to the fact that not everyone will be able to offer you the level of intimacy you need. Remember that good relationships tend to just flow, so be wary if it feels like an uphill battle getting to know them.

Think This:

"My own needs for intimacy are valid, and whether we're on the same page, in terms of how much affection we like, is an important point of compatibility for me."

Say This:

"As long as we're moving in the same direction, it's okay if we go at a slightly different pace."

"I'd like to be able to spend more time together."

"I really like you as a person, but I need more."

WHAT NEXT?

There's a lot of merit to taking things slowly; you get to know the real person and stand a chance at building a solid relationship rather than a short-lived romance. However, for a long-term relationship to be built, you need to spend time together and have a partner who is as willing as you are to let someone into their life.

They Keep Rescheduling Your Dates

Your first date or two seemed to go well; since then, you keep making plans, but something always comes up and they have to reschedule. You like them, and their reasons often seem genuine enough, but you're starting to feel like they're not respecting your time. How do you move forward if you're not sure whether they're in or they're out?

 Follow these steps to get started:

1 Consider whether this has happened more than once.
A one-off reschedule is understandable; sometimes life genuinely gets in the way of meeting. However, if someone is sincerely interested in you then they will always offer you a clear alternative and stick to the plan the next time around. If your date is constantly postponed due to their busy schedule, read the writing on the wall that says they're just not at the right stage in their life to give you what you need.

2 Stick to the original plan for the date, or at least a date you're comfortable with.
Were you excited to go out for dinner with them on Friday night, only for them to rain check at the last moment and invite you over to their house to hang out the next day instead? If you're looking for a committed relationship, don't just meet on their terms.

3 Ask yourself what kind of relationship you are looking for.
Flaky dates can be annoying. However, if you're just casually dating, and can avoid developing any expectations for the relationship, then you can probably afford to be more laissez-faire about rescheduling.

DON'T ALLOW YOURSELF TO BE CONSTANTLY CANCELED ON. The start of a relationship is about setting precedents. If you allow someone to continually cancel on you at the last minute, then you're not creating respect for your own time. Remember: If there's no respect, there's no real relationship there. If you compromise on everything because you don't want to lose someone, chances are they'll lose so much respect for you along the way that they'll end up being the one to walk away.

✔ HERE'S HOW

Even if you like them, maintain healthy boundaries around rescheduling. If it's a one-off and they seem genuinely bummed to not be able to meet, let it go. If, however, you're getting hit with a lot of vague excuses like, "Something's come up, if my work's not too busy next week I'll see if we can meet then," watch out. Notice if someone is meeting you halfway and respecting your time, or squeezing you in around every other commitment they have. Building a relationship is a two-way process, so unless they're also putting the effort in, this is a nonstarter.

Think This:

"The minimum I need from someone is that they're as willing as I am to build a relationship. Without this key ingredient there's a limit to how much I can do, so it's important for me to recognize when the effort isn't there and be prepared to walk away."

Say This:

"Just so you know, that's the last time I'm asking ;-)"

"It sounds like you've got a lot going on, let's leave it for now. Best of luck turning that project in."

"I can't do tomorrow, but maybe we can try again next week."

WHAT NEXT? ⟶

Don't settle for being constantly canceled on. By having healthy boundaries, you'll either make someone more attracted to you or move on faster from a relationship that was never going to work out.

Chapter 4

LIVING

TOGETHER

Moving in together is a huge gear change for your relationship: The days of sexy dinner dates have been replaced by seeing each other in your pajamas on a daily basis. At this stage in your relationship the honeymoon period may be over, and you may find yourself bogged down with the realities of day-to-day life as a couple. In fact, between organizing who does the dishes and laundry, arguing over what kind of sofa to choose, and deciding where to live, you may feel like the romance has taken a back seat.

This chapter will help you to deal with the ups and downs of building a life together—from the mundane daily choices you have to make (like who does the cooking every night) to the bigger obstacles that can present themselves as you get to know one another on a deeper level. Maybe your partner has been unfaithful and you're unsure if your relationship can ever be the same. Or perhaps you're the one suddenly getting cold feet and wondering, "Is this it?" If you feel like you're driving past a relationship signpost that says, "Last chance to exit is here," this chapter will empower you to make the right decision for you.

You Don't Agree on Where to Live

Things are really getting serious now! However, if you have very different ideas about where you should live, this relationship milestone may start to feel more like a hurdle.

 **Follow these steps to get started:**

1 Consider how important it is to you to get your way.
They want to move to be closer to family; you want to keep your commute to work short. Both are very valid reasons for wanting to live somewhere. Instead of invalidating their preferences ("but we see your family all the time!"), listen to them and think long and hard about just how important getting your way is to you. Keep considering how much of a deal-breaker it is to move to an area that's not your first choice.

2 Drop the subject for a while.
When you're at a deadlock in an argument, walk away from the table for a while. Arguments that drag on and on can affect the quality of your relationship together; and if your relationship becomes less enjoyable, your partner is going to be less willing to compromise. Set a timeline of a couple of months to drop the subject and instead focus on strengthening your relationship. Hopefully when this subject comes back around, you'll both be more amenable to figuring out a solution.

3 Take time to thoroughly understand each other's point of view.
Have you even bothered to go and check out houses in the areas they like? Have they spent the day in the area you love? When something's unknown, it is easier to dislike. Rather than reaching broad, sweeping conclusions ("that area doesn't even have a sushi place!"), check it out, and keep an open mind.

DON'T SEE THIS AS A HUGE ISSUE IN YOUR RELATION- SHIP: "NO BIG DEAL" (NBD) IT. This means that you don't make this argument bigger than it is. Avoid catastrophizing ("We're never going to agree!"). So you haven't immediately agreed on where to live, but you will probably resolve this in time: Don't make this issue bigger than the relationship itself.

✓ HERE'S HOW

Is there any chance there's a third option here that you could both be happy with? Is there an area halfway that you could check out? Or could you do a short-term rental in each of your chosen areas to see which one works out better for you? If one of you ends up compromising on the area, can that person have more say in the kind of property you end up in? Think outside the box and see this as a problem you can solve as a team.

Think This:	**Say This:**
"This disagreement is temporary." Focus on the fact that a solution will present itself sooner or later. Don't get so caught up on being right that you get in the way of yourself being happy.	"How about we spend a day checking out both areas to get more intel?" "I do understand why that's important to you." "Is there another option here that we haven't thought of yet?"

WHAT NEXT?

Right now you might be at an impasse over your zip code, but there will be a glorious time in the future when you've reached an agreement... provided you stay open-minded to some compromise.

You Need to Figure Out Household Finances Together

Getting onto the same page financially will help you to avoid conflict in the future. Especially as you move further into your partnership (marriage, children, etc.), your finances will become more intertwined.

 **Follow these steps to get started:**

1 **Be candid with one another about your finances.**
You know that credit card bill that keeps getting bigger? At some stage (preferably sooner rather than later) you're going to have to lay out your financial status to your partner. Unfortunately, a lot of big life goals (whether it's having kids or traveling around the world on a Harley-Davidson) all require money to make them happen. Bad debt or bad credit ratings can make accomplishing your life goals harder. Be open with each other about your finances, and work as a team to become better with money.

2 **Work out what you spend your money on, and look out for savings.**
One of the perks of being a couple is that it's much less expensive than being single. Rent? Split it! Being a couple will make it easier for you to save. To help work this out, get a spreadsheet going. Work out what you spend your money on, how much you can realistically save every month, and how long it will take you to reach your savings goals.

3 **Educate yourselves.**
Being great at managing money is something you probably didn't get taught at school, so see learning about your finances as a new pet project you can embark on together. There are great blogs, podcasts, and non-scary ways to learn how you can get much smarter with your money.

DON'T MERGE ALL YOUR FINANCES OVERNIGHT; THIS IS A PROCESS. Just like how you know you shouldn't send money to a person you've just met online, you don't need to throw all your finances together immediately. And it should raise a big red flag if your new partner is asking for a loan. Instead, start small on learning how to manage your spending together: Figure out how to split the weekly grocery bill, how you pay rent, and who picks up the bill at a restaurant before you open a joint bank account.

HERE'S HOW

When it comes to figuring out your finances together, remember that eventually (if things go well) you will become a unit. You don't need to be in a rush to get there, but there will come a time when you stop seeing it as "my money" and "your money." It's destined to become "our money" as you work more and more together as a team.

Think This:

"We both contribute to this relationship." Avoid feeling bad or inadequate if your partner earns more than you. It doesn't mean that you work less hard than they do, or that your work is less meaningful; it simply means that some sectors are rewarded more financially than others. If you're the higher-earning partner, also empathize that even if your partner doesn't earn as much as you, it doesn't mean that their work is any less valid.

Say This:

"Okay, let's get that spreadsheet started."

"We'll get there in the end, if we work together."

"I want to work out a contribution from both of us that's fair."

WHAT NEXT?

Working toward a savings goal doesn't sound all that romantic, but it can be one of your best life achievements—one that's easier to accomplish together.

You Need to Distribute Household Chores

It's not a sexy word, but "domesticity" is a key part of long-term relationships. Remember that you're now starting to operate as a crack team, tackling all of life's challenges together, such as how to correctly load the dishwasher. Between establishing your careers, and maybe making babies, how you divide up the household chores is going to be a big part of your lives together.

 Follow these steps to get started:

1 Create a rotation chart.
It's not romantic, but it is highly practical. Work out a list of all the household chores (from laundry to the weekly trip for groceries) and then set days when each of you will complete them. Make one of you accountable for successfully completing each household chore.

2 Praise your partner for completing a chore.
Yes, they stacked the dishwasher totally the wrong way, and *obviously* your way of loading it is far superior. However, after someone has tried to do the right thing, the last thing they need to hear is that they did it badly. Now is a great opportunity to create a positive feedback loop and praise your partner for doing the chores.

3 Openly discuss your frustrations with your partner.
Rather than assuming they haven't done the vacuuming just to spite you, have an open conversation with your partner about the division of chores. Some people don't mind a mess, some people's exes did all the heavy lifting, and some people still get their mom to do their laundry. You need to make your partner aware of what your expectations are.

DON'T TAKE ON MORE THAN YOU'RE HAPPY WITH AND WIND UP FEELING RESENTFUL. If you're standing there ironing a pile of clothes through gritted teeth, stop right there! You don't need to be a martyr for the chores you've completed. Don't just gripe that "if I don't do it, it's not going to get done"; start making your needs clear to your partner and give them the opportunity to help you.

✓ HERE'S HOW

Accept that domesticity is going to take time out of your relationship. It can't all be passionate romance when the reality is you both need to eat, and live somewhere clean. Yes, it can feel unromantic to talk about chores, but if it helps to avoid resentment from one partner who's doing more than their fair share, it's well worth it.

Think This:

"If we both feel like the division of chores is fair, it's going to help our relationship." Good chore distribution = a better sex life. If you ever needed an incentive to get your chore list under control, this is it.

Say This:

"Let's put together a rotation chart for chores."

"Thank you so much for doing the vacuuming. I hate that job."

"We're both really busy at the moment, so perhaps we should invest in a cleaner?"

WHAT NEXT?

Your end goal here is to create harmony within your relationship. By organizing the basics of household chores as a team, you will open up more capacity for you both to feel satisfied in the relationship. Work together so you both feel that the way chores are divided up is fair, and recognize what the other partner contributes. Then, after that last load of laundry is done, it's sexy time.

You're Debating Getting a Pet Together

It's not quite a ring, but it's still a commitment. Getting a pet together would mean your lives are suddenly a lot more intertwined: You'll be sharing the time and financial commitment of looking after another being. It's not quite on the level of having a baby, but is it a step in that direction? And if you split up, who's going to get custody?

DO THIS *Follow these steps to get started:*

1 **Talk about how you're going to split responsibilities.**
If your pet gets sick, or needs to be vaccinated, who is going to pick up the bill at the vet? If you're getting a dog, who is responsible for their daily walks? Get this ironed out before you adopt your pet to save you conflict later.

2 **Think about what you'll do in the event of splitting up.**
First, do you think that's at all likely to happen? If so, you don't want a Band-Aid puppy (an attempt to "fix" or "save" the relationship) that will need rehoming if you eventually split. If you do break up, could shared custody be an option? Or would it make more sense for one of you to look after the pet full time? Agree on this (and, if possible, put in writing) before taking the next step.

3 **Consider whether there is a lower level of commitment to try first.**
If you're on the fence, or your relationship is up and down, could you try a smaller shared commitment first? Yes, house plants, pet fish, or a shared creative project aren't quite as cuddly, but they'll help you to test the water of how successfully you're able to share a responsibility like this before you up the stakes.

DON'T ASSUME THIS MEANS YOUR RELATIONSHIP IS HEADING IN ONE DIRECTION. Yes, both of you cooing over a new puppy might feel a lot like you're moving toward an actual baby sooner rather than later, but don't bank on your partner jumping to the same conclusion. Getting a pet together for you might mean a step toward a bigger commitment; for them, it could just be something fun to do.

 HERE'S HOW

Before you get a pet, you must get practical. Do you really have enough time to look after a pet? No one wants an anxious pooch staring out the window all day long when you're at work. Do you have enough disposable income to pick up those extra bills? Do you both agree on what kind of pet you want? Is where you live suitable for a pet? If you're both on the same page and genuinely have the bandwidth to take this next step, then looking after a pet can bring you even closer as a couple.

Think This:

"This is an opportunity to see how we handle a step up in our relationship." Like most relationship stages, you're about to get some feedback as to how well your relationship copes with this new, and more committed, phase. Do you grow closer together? Or does increased commitment show that cracks are there? Be extra careful with this next step, as it involves a living being that deserves proper care.

Say This:

"I thought since I work from home it could be manageable to get a puppy or kitten. What do you think?"

"How do you see us sharing responsibility for them?"

"Who will look after Duke when we go on vacation?"

WHAT NEXT?

This could be the start of taking your relationship to the next level, and seeing a new side of each other. It's not guaranteed, but if there's some serious admiration for how the other person cares for your pet, then this could mean you see your partner's parenting potential more clearly.

You Don't Agree On Who Is Going to Cook

When you were single, fixing meals was easy: some quick pasta, left-over pizza, or take-out sushi (with a large glass of wine) worked just fine. Now you're cohabiting and suddenly it makes sense to cook for two, but who takes on the chore? Do you split it down the middle? Is one of you unsure how to use any kitchen appliance beyond a micro-wave? How do you agree on who is going to cook?

 Follow these steps to get started:

1 Consider what each of you feels is fair.
In the age of the dishwasher, the old divide of "you do the cooking and I'll do the washing up" doesn't work out quite as equitably. You don't need to split the cooking fifty-fifty; you just need to feel that whatever arrangement you come to is fair.

2 Support your partner in learning new cooking skills.
If one of you is a borderline Michelin star chef, and the other gets flus-tered boiling an egg, it can feel obvious for the more experienced chef to cook. However, in the long run this isn't likely to be sustainable. Set a goal for the inexperienced cook to learn one simple dish a week, and heap praise on whatever they manage to rustle up.

3 If you're both tired, consider getting a food delivery service.
Nothing's worse than both of you stumbling through the door exhausted at the end of a long day and having a "who is more tired?" contest to decide who does the cooking. If both your jobs are very demanding, then get a meal preparation service, ready meals, or a lot of takeout to tide you over during this time-strapped period.

DON'T ASSUME THE OTHER PERSON IS GOING TO DO ALL THE COOKING. Even if they don't have a job, are a student, or have a job that you feel is less stressful than yours, this doesn't create an implicit agreement that they'll be taking on this chore. If you feel it's fairer that they do the cooking, you're going to need to have a conversation about it and verbally agree to that.

 HERE'S HOW

Cooking is another one of those annoying domestic tasks that takes up a lot of time. In fact, a huge part of your future relationship might be turning to the other person and asking, "So what do you feel like for dinner?" Cooking together can be romantic and fun, but over weeks, months, and years this experience might also start to feel like drudgery. Make sure this massive task doesn't fall entirely to one person, and don't be afraid to fall back on low-effort evening meals to see you through those challenging midweek nights. Save any elaborate cooking for the weekend.

Think This:	**Say This:**
"It takes time, effort, and energy to cook, so if my partner steps up to care for me in this way, I'm going to really thank them for whatever they make. (And I will absolutely not say a word if my eggs are overdone.)"	"Thank you, I appreciate you cooking." "Looks like we're going to have a busy few weeks at work. How can we make cooking easier?" "It doesn't matter how it turned out. I really like that you tried."

WHAT NEXT? ⟶

Sharing this age-old domestic task fairly will help both of you to feel appreciated. No one wants to become resentful of cooking after years of doing all the work. Divide this chore fairly, and recognize the efforts of whoever takes it on.

You're a Night Owl and They're an Early Bird (or Vice Versa)

Do you like working at night or staying up watching movies, and sleeping in on the weekends? This is great unless you've got a partner who likes waking up early to seize the day, and whose idea of a good time is an early night and a hot-water bottle. Or maybe you're the one hitting the hay early while your partner wants to keep the party going all night. If one of you is a night owl, and the other's an early bird, how do you make this work?

 **Follow these steps to get started:**

1 **Be flexible about how you spend your time.**
Accept that the other partner is on a different schedule than you are and don't pressure them into that early-morning hike, or late-night movie marathon, just because it's what you like to do.

2 **Recognize the benefits of being on opposing sleep cycles.**
If you eventually have children together, having someone on the early shift and someone else on the late-late shift can be very helpful. If you run a business together, well, that's nearly twenty-four-hour around-the-clock coverage! If there are chores to be done, then either the early bird or the night owl can be on duty while the other person rests.

3 **Understand that everyone is better after a good night's sleep.**
If you want to have an argument, speak to a tired person. You may see your partner's early nights, or late wakings, as a little boring, but they will be a better partner to you if they're allowed to get their z's.

DON'T SULK BECAUSE YOU MISS OUT ON SOME TIME IN BED TOGETHER. To start with, it may feel a bit weird for you to go to bed while your partner starts their work, but this is a small compromise to make. Just like how you don't have to have every single hobby in common to make a relationship work, you don't need to get up and go to bed at exactly the same times either.

HERE'S HOW

How long, and at what time, you want to sleep is in fact hereditary (look up "chronotypes" online for more information), so there's little point trying to change a night owl to an early bird and vice versa. In fact, there's little point in trying to change your partner, period. Instead, you're back to that important A-word for relationships: acceptance.

Think This:

"We don't need to spend every minute of the day together to have quality time." Make a decision to enjoy your solo time while they're sleeping, and to not be annoyed with them just because they have a different sleep schedule than you.

Say This:

"It's okay...it's important for you to get your rest."

"Good luck with your work. I'm going to go to bed."

"I actually enjoy some me-time in the mornings, but I can always come back to bed for a cuddle."

WHAT NEXT? ⟶

Being on opposite schedules isn't always a bad thing. That early morning veterinary appointment—that's an early bird's job! Who cleaned the kitchen after you went to bed? Thanks, night owl! Create harmony by reaping the benefits of your nearly 24-hour coverage of being awake.

You Need Some Space

The first question to ask here is, why? Has something happened? Are you finding being together claustrophobic? Get to the bottom of why you need space to establish just how much of it you need to take.

Follow these steps to get started:

1 **Consider whether you need space because something's happened.**
If you've had a big fight, or there's been an unexpected revelation, then you may need some headspace to process things. There may not be a timeline for how long this is going to take. However, you still need to communicate what you do know with your partner. Explain this isn't a breakup: It's about you having some time apart to work out your feelings.

2 **Consider whether you need space because you think you might prefer to be single.**
Are you suggesting "taking a break" because sneakily (admit it!) you'd like to see what it's like being single again? Yes, it's a convenient solution to have your partner wait for you while you "go figure things out" (read: go on some hot dates!), but this shows a lack of respect for your partner. Don't keep them on the hook as an option for you.

3 **Consider whether you need space because you feel trapped in the relationship.**
Ask yourself, "Is this a pattern for me?" Do you always enjoy relationships at the start then slowly find them more and more suffocating? If so, you may be someone who needs more independence in a relationship to function. Explain this to your partner rather than canceling plans and growing distant. Don't destabilize the relationship by just vanishing.

DON'T MAKE A RASH DECISION. Think carefully about why you need space. In a relationship, you have to focus on the apple not the worm: that's a person's good qualities over their minor imperfections. If you're nit-picking, this is probably less about them and more about you feeling uncomfortable with being close to someone.

 HERE'S HOW

When you take some space, you want to do it in a way that preserves the integrity of the relationship: Say why you need to take some space. Give a timeline for when they'll hear from you. Tell them what you need to be different in the future, don't just disappear.

Think This:	Say This:
"Taking space doesn't mean I'm emotionally checking out of this relationship. If I need to take space, this shouldn't be a surprise to my partner, and it's also my responsibility to communicate to them how I'm feeling."	"It's been a really stressful time and I need some space now to process things; I'm going to take a few days for myself, but I'll give you a call this weekend." "I have to be honest that I've been curious recently about what it would be like to be single, and because of that I don't think I can give this relationship my all." "I like a lot of space to feel calm and secure and I want to reassure you that it's nothing personal."

WHAT NEXT?

If your partner can't respect your need for space, and you wake up to twenty missed calls from them on your phone....Or if your partner feels insecure in the relationship because you've disappeared *again*....Or if you've decided that actually it's not so much space but being single that you really want....Then you've got your answer right there.

You Don't Like the Same Decor

You've moved in together, popped the champagne, and then discovered that they have the worst possible taste in decor. After years of you both living by yourselves, you're not used to compromise, but unless you want your home to be a real mishmash of styles, that's exactly what you're going to have to do.

 Follow *these steps to get started:*

1 **Try the three-two-one rule.**
Can't decide on what color to paint the walls? Ask your partner to choose three colors they like, you then choose two of those colors, and they choose the final one. Or vice versa. The goal here is to find a midway option that you can both agree on, and to keep any conversations about what to do as light and as playful as possible.

2 **Create a digital mood board where you both save styles you like.**
Allow this to build up over time and look out for areas where you converge. If one of you is naturally more design focused, try to engage your partner's interest in interiors with magazines, TV shows, and social media accounts. If they're still utterly disengaged, don't read this as a sign to just go ahead and do what you like; keep trying to consult them.

3 **Get a professional opinion.**
If you really, really can't agree, then get an impartial (again, *impartial*, not, say, your mom) interior designer to hear both of you out and find a solution that will keep both of you happy.

DON'T BRING A COMMITTEE OF FRIENDS (WHO ALL AGREE WITH YOU ABOUT DECOR) TO YOUR HOME. Everyone is entitled to their own opinions about interior design, and bullying your partner into agreeing with you will set you up for resentment further down the line. Make sure that it never becomes an argument about one person being right, and instead seek compromise.

 **HERE'S HOW**

Don't get stuck on the idea of winning. If you get everything your way, and all the decor is exactly how you'd like it to be, this isn't a good result. You don't want to be the person with better taste; you want to create a home that you can both live in and enjoy. Years down the line, you don't ever want to hear your partner say, "I always hated that couch."

Think This:	**Say This:**
"My partner's taste isn't inferior; it's just different." Compromise is the best solution here: Can you incorporate your styles together? Have different rooms you're both responsible for? Or go for a neutral decor as a halfway measure?	"Let me see what kind of things you like." "If we're both not sure about it, we probably shouldn't buy it." "It's just a paint color, and isn't that important."

WHAT NEXT?

What color you paint your walls isn't going to make or break your relationship. How you treat your partner when you don't agree on something is the important thing. If you need to be right, if you bully your partner, or if you belittle their choices, this is going to do a lot more damage to your relationship than tolerating a lamp shade that you don't love.

Your Partner Wants to Have People Over More Than You Do

Your partner is an extrovert. You love how warm, friendly, and sociable they are....Well, you did until you realized this meant a constant influx of people over to your home. Does there always seem to be an occasion to celebrate, and tidying up to do afterward? Are you starting to wonder if their best friend has moved in? Maybe you're craving personal space, or just some quality time as a couple—how do you compromise?

 **Follow these steps to get started:**

1 Set some healthy boundaries.
They may love the "open house" feeling, but it's also reasonable for you to need some personal space. Having their best friend as a permanent feature in your living room may be ruining your intimacy as a couple. Put some ground rules in place; for example, that you have to both agree in advance for people to come over.

2 Help your partner to understand that not everyone relaxes in the same way.
While they may feel energized by having a house party, you could feel drained by all the socializing. As much as you want to understand their need to celebrate important occasions as part of a big group, they also need to understand that for you, quality time means one-on-one.

3 Get them to be responsible for hosting.
Having people over can be fun, but it also requires a major upswing in domestic chores. Food has to be made, the house has to be cleaned, and then cleaned again. Someone will likely stain the couch. Don't silently do all the work and be left feeling more and more resentful.

DON'T NEGLECT YOUR OWN NEEDS. If you're naturally more of an introvert, you will probably enjoy having privacy, alone time, and one-on-one conversations. These needs are just as valid as those of someone who likes to be the life and soul of the party. Don't over-give to the point where you're emotionally exhausted and resentful.

HERE'S HOW

The solution here could be as simple as just having a conversation. Your partner may simply not realize that you're not enjoying having people over as much as they do. Help them to understand your needs for privacy and quiet time. Just as you might host a party to make them feel happy, they should also be equally ready to give you the alone time you need to feel restored.

<table>
<tr><td>Think This:</td><td>Say This:</td></tr>
<tr><td>"I can't expect my partner to like all of the same things as I do, or to intuitively understand my needs." Communicate, compromise, and if your partner constantly ignores your boundaries, then there's a bigger issue here than having different social preferences.</td><td>"I know it's important for you to see your friends, but I really need some downtime this weekend."

"Perhaps you can meet them at their place instead?"

"I need to have more quality time with you one-on-one."</td></tr>
</table>

WHAT NEXT?

This is a relationship problem with a lot of possible solutions: They could go to their friend's house or meet at a bar, or you could agree that Saturdays are a social day and keep Sundays for you as a couple. With this many good compromises available, there's no excuse for one person to force their idea of a good time onto the other.

You Think Your Partner Is Going Through Your Stuff

Did they just flinch as you walked in the room? Was your phone left unlocked? What about that old photo frame that you were sure was in a cupboard? It's not a nice feeling to have someone snooping in your personal space, especially if that person is your partner. So what do you do if you think your partner is going through your stuff?

 Follow *these steps to get started:*

1 **Put on your big person pants and have *that* conversation.**
Yes, it's going to be hard to tell your partner about your suspicions without being accusatory, but it's a conversation you need to have. Rather than entering into a secret battle where you change passwords, and they try to code-break them, it's time to talk to them about what they're doing and, more importantly, why.

2 **Make your boundaries clear.**
If your partner snoops through your phone and finds evidence of you cheating, who is wrong? Or are you both at fault? If you know there's no reason why they should be suspicious, can you explain that you'd rather they asked you about any concerns they have rather than going through your phone?

3 **Reassure your partner.**
Is there a reason your partner might be feeling especially insecure right now? Have you been unfaithful? Has your relationship lacked physical intimacy? Are they going through your things in a misguided attempt to get answers?

DON'T CHANGE YOUR PASSWORDS WITHOUT ANY OPEN COMMUNICATION ABOUT WHAT'S BEEN GOING ON. Tightening up your personal security may feel like the path of least resistance to stopping this from going any further, but your relationship may start to feel like war. You'll both have suspicions that haven't been aired, and this can create a toxic atmosphere.

 ## HERE'S HOW

Different couples have different attitudes toward privacy and passwords. Some people know all their partner's passwords, and to them this equals trust. Others give one another privacy as a way of giving trust. It doesn't matter what your exact setup for creating trust is, just that it exists. If your partner continually distrusts you (or you them), this will erode the happiness in your relationship. If your partner snoops, try to understand why, and be clear that this isn't acceptable to you.

Think This:

"If my partner is snooping, chances are they feel insecure and out of control. Is this something I can empathize with and help them to work through? Or is this a deal-breaker for me?" By looking through your things, your partner is looking for answers to something they can't work out about your relationship. Maybe their insecurities come from being cheated on in the past, or maybe they're to do with something that happened in your relationship. Focus less on the behavior and more on solving their underlying need for security.

Say This:

"I noticed that you'd checked my phone lately, and I wanted to understand why you felt like you needed to do that?"

"I need to feel trusted by you."

"I know things haven't always been easy in your past, but I want you to feel really secure in our relationship."

WHAT NEXT?

Do your best to understand your partner; be open, communicate, and try to resolve where their instinct to snoop is coming from. If they keep trying to solve their insecurities by snooping, it may be time to walk away.

You Want to Talk about Marriage

The M-word is on your mind. Perhaps friends and family keep asking or maybe it's you who wants to take the next step, but you're not sure your partner feels the same. Short of a proposal, what do you do? And how do you handle it if your partner doesn't want the same things?

 **Follow these steps to get started:**

1 Talk about marriage before popping the question.
A surprise proposal is wonderful, but check that your partner is on the same page first. If you're both moving in the same direction, then the M-word should be part of an ongoing conversation about your life goals.

2 Kick-start the conversation by telling your partner about what you want.
It can be awkward to try and weave "So what do you think about marriage?" into an unrelated conversation. It will feel more natural for you to express your views first. Explain that marriage is something you've always wanted, or that it's not something that's important to you, or any other view you have. Your partner should feel more comfortable expressing their opinion if you lead the way.

3 Watch out for avoidance on their part.
It can be workable if your partner has different views on marriage (more on this later), but watch out if they eternally dodge the subject. Their silence around the subject is telling, and you also deserve a direct answer.

DON'T CAVE IN TO PRESSURE TO MARRY IF THAT'S NOT SOMETHING YOU WANT AS A COUPLE. When you were single it was a constant grilling about why you were still single. Now it's all about when are you going to get married, and even if you do, your family is sure to clamp on the pressure for babies. Constantly justifying your life choices is tiring, right? Take comfort in the fact that most people think they're just "showing an interest"; it's not meant to feel like an interrogation. Keep your response to them short, sweet, and enigmatic. Say, "That's actually not something we're planning on doing" or "I guess you'll have to wait and see."

✅ HERE'S HOW

Marriage is an emotionally charged subject. You may both have developed firm ideas about marriage early on in life, and now you're trying to work out if they line up. Some compromises will be easier to make than others (like how many wedding guests you have), while it may be very challenging to overcome a fundamental difference of opinion (you want to get married and they don't). If you hit a deadlock, do your best to hear your partner out, and express your fears too.

Think This:	**Say This:**
"I need to be open about what I want. The best partner(s) for me will be heading in the same direction."	"I've actually always wanted to get married."
	"I've never seen myself getting married, though I do want to have a lifelong committed relationship."
	"I'm not at a stage in my life, and may never be at that stage, where I can make that level of commitment."

WHAT NEXT?

Plenty of couples choose not to marry and that suits them, but if you crave that level of commitment and it's not something your partner wants, you'll need to work out if you can compromise. And if you can't compromise, can you truly accept their choices without feeling resentful further down the line?

You Are Considering Buying a House Together

There are a lot of commitments you can make to your partner, and buying a house together is one of the most significant. It's an investment not only of your wealth, but also in the promise of a future together.

Follow *these steps*
to get started:

1 **Discuss how you are going to organize the mortgage between you.**
Is one of you the higher earner, or does one of you have a better credit rating? This may influence who applies for the mortgage, or you can apply as co-borrowers even if you're not married. However, if your partner is applying for the mortgage on their own, and you're not going to be on the property title, you should seek legal advice about your rights in case you separate from your partner.

2 **Have a clear-cut idea of how you're going to pay for this.**
Is someone fronting the deposit? Are you going to share mortgage repayments? Do you feel your financial contribution to the property is clearly reflected in its ownership rights?

3 **Consider whether it is important for you to get married before you take this step.**
It's increasingly common for unmarried couples to buy properties together; however, if you're traditional at heart, you may want to think about getting hitched first. Houses are expensive and time-consuming, so that may wipe any wedding plans off the immediate agenda.

DON'T RUSH INTO THE IDEA OF BUYING A HOME TOGETHER WITHOUT UNDERSTANDING THE LEGALITIES BEHIND IT. Yes, it all sounds very exciting on paper, but, particularly if you're unmarried, things could get complicated if you split up. Agree ahead of time on how you're going to divide up the house if you do part ways, and if either of you will keep living there. Educate yourself and get legal advice before jumping in.

 HERE'S HOW

There's a lot to work out before taking this next step. What's your budget? Where are you looking to buy? Who's on the property title? What will you do if you split up? How will you manage monthly costs? If you've got a strong and mature relationship (and probably a few budget spreadsheets to boot), then this may well feel like the logical next step. However, it's not the only step to becoming more committed, so make sure you feel 100-percent secure with your partner before you take this next step.

Think This:

"I'm excited about this next step; however, I owe it to myself as an individual to make sure that legally I know where I stand. I hope that we'll never have to break up, but if by chance we do, I know it will make things easier to have how we divide our assets worked out ahead of time with the help of a lawyer."

Say This:

"How do you see us dividing things up if we split?"

"I'm really excited about buying a place together; it's a big step so I think we should talk about our other life goals before we make it."

"What does your dream house look like?"

WHAT NEXT? ⟶

Hopefully after a few chats with your lawyer and mortgage broker, you'll be celebrating by getting frisky on the kitchen counter. This is really starting to look like you've found the committed, happy relationship you deserve!

You're Getting Cold Feet

When you first met, you were convinced that you'd met "The One." You had a great connection and wanted to spend every moment together. However, as time's gone on, you've felt doubt creeping in. Some things that they do are starting to really bug you, and now it feels like you're on a one-track train journey to a destination that you're not sure you want to reach. Are you just getting cold feet? Or is there a legitimate reason here for you to back off?

 Follow *these steps to get started:*

1 Identify when these doubts began.
Have you been worried for a long time about an aspect of your partner's behavior? Have friends said their alarm bells are ringing? Are you feeling a sense of dread in the run-up to the wedding day? If so, you might have feelings about getting married that you need to listen to. If possible, take some time away from your partner to reflect on what you really want. On the other hand, if your cold feet were triggered by an avalanche of wedding planning, then it's possible that these pre-wedding jitters are about the stress of organizing the day.

2 Consider how fast things are moving.
How well have you gotten to know your partner? If it's been a whirlwind romance, your nerves could be telling you to slow it down. A good partner will understand if you need more time before taking such a big step.

3 Consider whether there is a need that you don't agree on.
Does one of you want children and the other doesn't? Do you have different religious beliefs? Is there drug or alcohol abuse in the relationship? Don't leave it to the altar to have these important conversations.

DON'T BELIEVE THAT YOU'RE TRAPPED. Even if you've ordered the wedding cake, you are not a hostage to this situation. Yes, you may lose some money and let some people down. Yes, if you want to get married one day, you will have to go out and meet someone else (this part may be more fun than you think). However, these compromises are much easier to make now than later down the line. So, if you have concerns that you can't easily move past, remember that it's not too late to change your mind.

HERE'S HOW

Can you talk to your partner? In a good partnership you should be able to communicate your fears and seek reassurance. Opening up to your partner should remind you of exactly the reason why they're the one you want to commit to for the long term. If you're fearful of talking to them, then this is a clear signal that your concerns are well founded, and you'll want to find another confidante to talk it through with instead.

Think This:	Say This:
"Is how I'm feeling now about the stress of planning a wedding, or am I genuinely concerned about the relationship?"	"I've been feeling anxious about our wedding. Can you help me with more of the planning?"
	"I still really want to be with you, but I'd like to take this next step more slowly."
	"There are a few things that have been playing on my mind. Can we talk it through?"

WHAT NEXT?

Getting married is a major life transition, so it's normal to feel some nerves. However, make sure these nerves are about whether the florist will turn up on time, and not about whether you've made the right choice of partner. There's no rush to reach the destination of being married.

You're Comparing Your Relationship to Other People's

You're happy-ish in your relationship. Things are fine; they're normal. But you're starting to worry about whether what you have is enough for you. Your friends' partners always seem to do things a little bit better: They make an effort on their birthdays, whisk them away on foreign vacations, and post envy-inducing pictures on social media. Is your relationship *really* normal, or are you settling for less?

 **Follow these steps to get started:**

1 Recognize the impact of social media scrolling.
That perfectly staged picture of your friends on a gondola in Venice? That's not real life! If you feel less content every time you look on social media, the problem could be with your scrolling rather than your relationship. Try a digital detox and see if that changes how you feel.

2 Consider whether your friends are open with you about the imperfections in their relationships.
Do you feel like you can confide in each other? Here's the deal: No one's relationship is perfect. If you feel like every time you open up to your friends about your relationship they negatively compare your partner to theirs, this could be saying more about your choice of friends than it says about your romantic partners.

3 Ask yourself what your partner does bring to your relationship.
Not everyone expresses their love in the same way. Is your partner less about the feet-sweeping gestures, and more about being a day-to-day good partner? Romantic gestures are nice, but they're nowhere near as important as a partner who consistently treats you with kindness and respect.

DON'T COMPARE YOUR BEHIND-THE-SCENES FOOTAGE TO THEIR HIGHLIGHTS REEL. You know that picture from Venice isn't the full story, right? Look behind that posed moment and there's probably a litany of travel-related disasters, from food poisoning, to airport stress, to a leaky sink in the hotel room. Instead of focusing on how wonderful someone else's relationship *seems*, focus instead on how happy you are day to day in yours.

HERE'S HOW

Have you tried to be the change? Rather than expecting your partner to be solely responsible for bringing novelty and excitement to your relationship, think instead about what you can plan and do to get your needs met. Perhaps your partner doesn't have a romantic bone in their body, but is very happy to go along with whatever you want to plan. Yes, it's not quite as exciting this way around, but it might be more realistic, and help you to get some of your needs met. If you're naturally more of a planner than your other half, take up this role.

Think This:	**Say This:**
"Instead of expecting my love life to be a 24/7 fairy tale, I'm going to work with my partner on how we can keep our relationship fun and enriching."	"I've planned a fun date night for us this weekend."
	"Do you ever have doubts about your relationship?"
	"Thank you for taking the trash out."

WHAT NEXT? ⟶

If you constantly feel let down by your partner, it might be that you're settling for less, and you need to move on. However, if your pangs of envy are related to scrolling social media or spending time with a friend who can't show any vulnerability, then these are the relationships that you really need to examine.

Your Partner Wants to Move and You Don't Want To

You're happy where you are, but your partner isn't. You like your neighborhood, but your partner has an itch to move on that they really need to scratch. Why can't they be as content as you? You want to support their dreams but not at the expense of the stability of your relationship.

 Follow these steps to get started:

1 Try to identify where their need is coming from.
If you're happy as you are, but your partner feels a strong desire for change, can you listen to their reasons and try to empathize with them? Have they stuck it out in a job they hate for too long and want to move to seek out new career opportunities? Do they have a sick parent far away who needs care? Understanding where they're coming from will help you to empathize with them, and not automatically judge their decision as irrational or selfish.

2 Consider whether this is a pattern.
Has this come up for you before in your relationship? Do you prefer stability, while your partner needs more stimulation than you do? Did their restlessness not bother you in the early days, but now that you have commitments together it feels jarring? Is there a chance this idea will pass, or is their need to change part of who they are?

3 Look for a compromise.
Maybe there's a midpoint destination you could move to? Could you both take a sabbatical from work to test out living in a new location before committing?

DON'T IMMEDIATELY SHOOT DOWN THEIR IDEAS. Their suggestion to move ("What?! We just re-did the kitchen!") could surprise you, and immediately make you feel anxious. However, steer clear of judging their plans as selfish, petty, or unviable. Even if you're sure you can't get on board with this, you still need to hear each other out.

 HERE'S HOW

If you're faced with an unwanted suggestion to change things up, do your best to keep an open mind. Change can feel intimidating, but hear out your partner for their reasons for wanting to do so. Work out between you if there's a compromise that could be made. You may not feel comfortable to make a radical change overnight (and your partner shouldn't expect you to be), but you can be open-minded to finding a middle ground.

Think This:	**Say This:**
"Their idea to change things up scares me. I'll be open with them about how I feel, but I'm also going to challenge myself not to focus on worst-case scenarios. Instead, can we try some blue sky thinking to find a third-way solution that meets both our needs?"	"I hear that you really want to do this, and I want to understand where that's coming from." "Right now the idea of a fundamental life change sounds scary, but I'm open to talking about it." "Is there a way we can try out what you want to do before committing to it as a couple?"

WHAT NEXT?

Wanting a change of scene is a lot simpler when you are single. Now there are at least two of you to consider. Working together as a partnership, you've got to strive to meet both your needs, and that can get tricky when they're not aligned. Find ways to test the water, and give yourself time to make this decision. If moving isn't workable for you, is there another way you can get your partner's need for a change-up met?

Chapter 5

BUILDING A LONG-TERM RELATIONSHIP

When you think about relationships, the first things that come into your mind might be dinner dates, minibreaks, and the moment you say, "I do." These moments are defining but fleeting. When you choose a partner for the long term, you're also choosing a teammate to accompany you through life's challenges. Who is the person who's going to be by your side as you deal with a bereavement, or discover that having kids is turning out to be a lot more challenging than you thought?

This chapter is about the big stuff. It's about building a family, discussing what your future holds, and rekindling a sex life that has become a thing of the past. It's about how to stay in a loving, committed relationship when you're not feeling appreciated by your partner, or when the memory of your ex is still on your mind. It's about how to choose to stay in love and build the happy, long-term partnership you deserve.

Your Sex Life Is Boring

There are plenty of reasons why it could have gone from red-hot twice a day to missionary position on your birthday: You know each other better now, you have kids, you have no free time, you don't feel attractive. Whatever the reason, a boring sex life will leave you both feeling unsatisfied, and ultimately lead to the question, "Is something missing here?"

 Follow *these steps*
to get started:

1 Know that just because it's boring now, doesn't mean it's going to be boring forever.
Relationships don't stay the same; they ebb and flow. Yes, it may be tricky to recapture the excitement you had before you'd helped your partner remove an ingrown hair, but that doesn't mean you're never going to have great sex again. Avoid defeatist phrases like, "I guess that's the end of that…"

2 Examine what's getting in the way of you having great sex.
Rather than your boring sex life being about a lack of mutual attraction, is it about circumstance? Is someone working long hours? Do you have small children? Is it possible to cut yourselves some slack for not having the best sex ever?

3 Spice it up, at your own pace.
If you're in a dry spell, it can feel incongruous to whip out sex toys. You might want to start with the basics: spend quality time together, turn your phones off more, dress up more, take a vacation. By restoring the intimacy levels in your relationship, it will set the stage for you both to be as open-minded (okay, as kinky) as you were when you first met.

DON'T BLAME YOUR PARTNER. When the sex is bad, people start to feel rejected. From this space of rejection, it's easy to lash out: to blame your partner for neglecting you, to accuse them of being with someone else, to belittle their sexuality... but don't blame your partner. Even if they're the one who is disinterested in sex, try to understand why.

 HERE'S HOW

Get your independence back. Good sex starts with yourself, and if your sex life has become too routine, it's up to you to shake it up. If you've been with your partner a while, it can be tempting to confuse them with a piece of furniture—they're just always there! How can you feel more excitement for them again? Would it be good to spend more time apart? Can you help them to sleep, exercise, or shower more so they feel sexier? Can you talk to them about your fantasies?

Think This:

"Is this a barometer of something else that's happening, or not happening, in our relationship?" Sex is a way people communicate, and if your sex life has dried up, it could be telling you something about your relationship as a whole. Often if you're not feeling happy (either with yourself or with your partner), your body will speak that language before you can verbalize it. Get to the root of what's stopping you from finding one another sexy. Is it circumstance or is it something deeper?

Say This:

"Let me take the kids today so you can have some time for yourself."

"We're tired, we're overworked, we're stressed, but our relationship is good; we just need to figure out how to nurture it more."

"I think it's really sexy when..."

WHAT NEXT? ⟶

Great sex in long-term relationships is possible, but it's not a given. Your relationship requires nurturing now, and that's okay.

Your Sex Drives Aren't In Sync

One of you wants sex as much as possible. The other one could take it or leave it. If you've got mismatched libidos, how do you make it work without one partner feeling deprived and the other fed up with the constant demands?

 **Follow these steps to get started:**

1 Have sex when both partners want to have sex.
If you're the higher-sexed partner, you're probably thinking, "Well, that means we will *never* have sex." Before you totally write off this idea, let's bring this back to associations: If your partner's association with sex is being emotionally detached from the experience because they didn't really want to go there, this will equal less sex in the long run. How can you work with your partner for the associations they have with sex to be positive?

2 Consider whether there are any easy fixes to help you sync up your desires.
Is there something that's holding back, or exacerbating, either partner's desire for sex? By fixing this bigger issue, could you get more in sync? For instance, does one partner crave sex as a release from a stressful job or need it to validate them? Does the other partner close off because they don't feel their emotional needs are taken care of? Can you start a non-blaming dialogue to get to the root of the problem?

3 Address any other sexual problems.
Is the issue bigger than mismatched sex drives? Are there other parts of your sex life that aren't working for you both that are putting a damper on sex altogether? Do you need to speak to a doctor or sexual therapist?

DON'T LABEL YOUR PARTNER FOR THEIR DIFFERENT LIBIDO. Calling them "sex-crazed" or "frigid" isn't going to help anyone. Don't blame your partner: This is a problem that you have to solve as a team.

HERE'S HOW

Go into problem-solving mode and see if there's changes in your lifestyle or a deeper understanding of your partner's sexual needs that will help. Approach this from a place of empathy and with a willingness to compromise. If a balance of meeting each other's needs really can't be struck, you could always consider ethical non-monogamy (where you both agree not to be sexually exclusive to one another) or parting ways on good terms.

Think This:	**Say This:**
"Their level of desire toward me isn't personal to anyone but them." If you're not having as much sex as you'd like, you may feel flat-out rejected. If you're feeling pressured to have more sex than you'd like, you may feel objectified. Remember that, for the most part, your partner's sex drive has to do with them, not you.	"I feel like we haven't connected much sexually recently and wanted to check in with how you feel." "I feel close to you when we have sex, but kissing and naked cuddles are also nice." "I need more time to get in the right zone for sex, and it's hard when I have a deadline hanging over me."

WHAT NEXT? ⟶

There's a good chance that with conscious effort and communication (which every single relationship you have will need), you'll be able to get this back on track. If you can't, and your needs feel too far apart, or one partner no longer desires to have sex, then there's a bigger conversation you can have about choosing ethical non-monogamy, acceptance, or potentially breaking up.

You Want to Break Up

"I want to break up!" is too easy to say in the heat of an argument, but it can be hard for a relationship to recover from. So before you make this big decision, let's look at what's motivating you, and if it's the right thing to do.

 Follow *these steps to get started:*

1 **Ask yourself whether this is about breaking up or whether it is a cry for help.**
Sometimes when people scream, "I just can't be with you anymore!" what they're really trying to say is "My needs are being constantly neglected and I need you to realize how strongly I feel about this!" So are you really at the "packing up my bags" phase or is this a protest? If it is a protest, is there a better way you can communicate what you need to be happy?

2 **Look for a pattern.**
Be honest: Is your relationship more on and off than a light switch? Are you in a toxic, but highly addictive, cycle of breaking up one minute and having a passionate reconciliation the next? If so, you're not really breaking up, are you? You're just starting this cycle all over again.

3 **If you decide this is the best thing for you, make it kind but clear.**
People don't function well when there's a lack of clarity or no explanation given. So unless you are fearful of your partner (in which case, contact a domestic abuse support service to help you leave safely), be prepared to put on those big person pants and have a conversation about your reasons for leaving.

DON'T STAY IN A RELATIONSHIP OUT OF OBLIGATION.
There's never a good time to break up with someone, but you're not doing them any favors by staying with them when you've already emotionally checked out. Being single means you're one step away from finding a great relationship; when you're in the wrong relationship, you're two steps away.

✓ HERE'S HOW

Your partner deserves an explanation, and the opportunity to ask questions: This is a dialogue not a monologue. They also deserve clarity, so don't continue to message them like you're still together, or have sex because you both feel lonely. Especially don't say things like, "I need some time to clear my head, but I'll come back for you when I'm ready" when you have no intention of doing so.

Think This:

"I'm going to get mentally prepared to doubt my decision, but I will remain strong." No matter how sure you are, there will come a day, a week, or a month when you'll miss the other person. See this as an inevitable part of breaking up, and don't respond (at least initially) to a knee-jerk reaction to get back together.

Say This:

"I really care about you, but I have to be honest that I don't want to do this anymore."

"I know you don't see this the same way now, but it's important for you to know that I won't change my mind. I'm not saying this to be cruel; I want you to have the best chance possible to move on."

"I'm sorry. I didn't mean that I wanted to break up. I said that because I was hurting, and I need us to work on our relationship."

WHAT NEXT? ⟶

You don't just get one shot at love in your life. Even if this hasn't worked out, starting over now doesn't put you back on square one: You now have a clearer idea of what you need in a partner and the chance to be happier than ever before.

Your Partner Is Being Abusive

Things haven't been right for a while.... Perhaps they were never right. Do you dread the minutes counting down before your partner returns home from work? Are their insults subtle ("being chubby looks good on you") or are they more overt ("you're just so stupid sometimes!"). What do you do if your partner is being abusive?

 *Follow these steps to get started:*

1 Keep a list of all the times their behavior is questionable.
If you're being gaslighted, your own sense of reality may be shaken by your partner's manipulation. Do they tell you you're being too sensitive? That they would never have said that? When you have a persuasive abuser in front of you, it can be hard to tell black from white. Write down examples of times you've felt their behavior was abusive to keep your own reality in check.

2 Confide in friends and family.
Ignore your partner saying it's inappropriate to discuss your relationship with anyone else. If your partner isn't supportive of your social relationships ("your friends don't really like you...") then you need those relationships more than ever.

3 Make a plan to get out.
The abuse isn't going to stop; in fact, it may get worse. You can't "save" your partner. It's time to save yourself and any dependents you have. Get a plan together with friends and family, and contact a domestic abuse support service. Today. Not tomorrow, or after you've gotten the car washed, *today*.

DON'T EXPECT THAT THEY'RE GOING TO CHANGE. They may have asked for one last chance, or almost bullied you into counseling, but you need to accept they're not going to change. The person you knew during the honeymoon phase doesn't really exist; the person you're with today represents the real relationship.

HERE'S HOW

Once you've begun to accept that you need to leave, a domestic abuse support service will help take you through the steps to help you do so safely. You will need to rehearse your exit plan. Feeling like you have nowhere to go will just prolong the abuse. Be ready to go at a moment's notice. Memorize useful contacts and keep them updated on your plans. Abuse can often escalate significantly at the end of a relationship, so you'll also want to consider how you can cut ties with your abuser after you've left. Can you change your cell phone number? Keep your new address secret? Take legal action? (If you do need to take legal action there may well be legal aid you can apply for to cover costs in this situation.) You can and will be happy. Protecting yourself today is your first step toward that goal.

Think This:

"Being honest with myself now, things aren't getting better, are they?" Think back to the start of the relationship: Was it better, did it get worse, did they say it would get better and it got worse again? Face up to the reality that this is one situation that is never going to change.

Say This:

"Even though I think I love this person, I need to preserve myself."

"Every time I think it's getting better, it doesn't. I have to break the cycle and get out."

"Who can help me to get out safely and start over?"

WHAT NEXT? ⟶

One day you'll look back on this and you will be thankful to your past self for being brave and getting out. There are a lot of great possibilities for your future; take the first step toward them today.

You Are Fighting...a Lot

Gone are the days of them calling you "baby." Every word you say starts an argument. When did your relationship fall apart? And is there any way to turn back the clock, or is it too late?

 **Follow these steps to get started:**

1 Ask whether you are fighting with each other or they are fighting with you.
This can be a very tricky distinction to make. To start to see things clearly, question your intentions: Do you try to listen, make them happy, and take what they say to heart? If nothing you do is ever good enough, and you're walking on eggshells trying not to trigger an outburst, refer to the previous section, Your Partner Is Being Abusive.

2 Push the reset button.
When you've been arguing a lot, you can get stuck on being right, on winning, on putting your foot down. How do you break this cycle and hit reset? Being aware you're in it is a good first step. Next try to change your setting. If an argument starts, get up and move. Don't have a standoff around your kitchen counter; go for a walk around the block. Change up the setting to try and get a reset on how you're relating to one another.

3 Consider whether you can better empathize with them.
Solving this argument will start with both parties feeling like they're able to be heard. What if you're doing this already and are tired of playing peacemaker? Then it could be time to change tack and put down some firm boundaries instead.

DON'T TRY ETERNALLY. It is good to work through things and not turn tail at the first sign of trouble, but you also have to know when to walk away. If they're not meeting you halfway, if they won't go to counseling, or if they are in any way abusive: Enough is enough.

HERE'S HOW

No one is perfect, and, to an extent, arguments are normal (even healthy!) in relationships. However, if open and direct communication has turned into sniping, petty arguments, and a full-blown power struggle, things need to change. Is there a third party who you can talk to about what you're going through? Can you do something together that will help you to remember why you fell in love? Is there a silly code word ("bananas!") you can shout when things get heated? And if all else fails, is there a chance here for you to be happier apart?

Think This:	**Say This:**
"As much as I'm frustrated with them, I also acknowledge that I haven't been perfect. How can we be kinder to one another?"	"I wanted to say, without reservation, that I'm really sorry."
	"I know we've been fighting a lot lately, but I love you and I want us to work through this."
	"Bananas! Bananas! Bananas!"

WHAT NEXT? ⟶

Relationships are constantly changing. Whether it's through conscious effort as a couple or with the help of a licensed therapist, there's every chance you can exit this difficult patch and return to happiness again. It's good to know what's possible. It's also possible that you make your peace that you can't try any harder, and that it's time to part. Either way, focus on the fact that you will be happy again.

Your Partner's Been Unfaithful

Before, it might have been a lipstick mark on someone's shirt collar or a crumpled number on a handkerchief. Now cheating could be secretly re-installing a dating app "to see what's out there," or sending a flirty message on social media. Or it could be that one person thought you were exclusive, but the other wasn't at that stage yet. Whatever way it happens, infidelity hurts.

Follow these steps to get started:

1 Consider whether you are on different pages about commitment.
Was your partner cheating because there was uncertainty about your status as a couple? Had you assumed because the relationship had become physical that exclusivity was implied? Had you deleted your dating app ages ago, so figured they were on the same page? This might not be all over yet. Have an open conversation about commitment and see if you can move forward.

2 Ask yourself if this is a deal-breaker for you.
If it is, walk. There is more than one person who can make you happy.

3 Understand it's not impossible to move on from this; it's just difficult.
Many couples experience infidelity and move on from it. There's no rule for how you deal with this. Maybe it will help you to understand why your partner was unfaithful; maybe it won't. Maybe you'll need some space, a friend to talk to, a promise that it will never happen again, or couples counseling to work through it. What will help you move on?

DON'T TRY TO FIND OUT EVERY DETAIL. After you get over the initial shock of finding out they were unfaithful, you'll probably want to go mining for every detail you can get your hands on. Was that the first time they'd cheated? How often did it happen? Be careful of trying to find out more details because you're hurting, and, on some strange level, you want to hurt more.

HERE'S HOW

You're at a fork in the road here: Leave the relationship or work toward accepting it. If you leave, make your exit quickly; don't stick around long enough to feel confused. If you decide you want to keep working on your relationship, know that the end destination you're heading for is acceptance. You want there to be a day in the future when this doesn't define your relationship, and you both have a clean slate.

Think This:

"It's not about me." Your immediate reaction might be to think that it's because you'd put on a few pounds, because your sex life wasn't as good as it used to be, or because you're not blond. Don't look for the "why" in how *you* are; the "why" is going to come from them. Were they feeling unloved, bored, like they wanted to feel young again? The reason isn't going to be as simple as "you weren't good enough," so don't allow yourself to believe that this is what their infidelity was all about.

Say This:

"I don't need to know the details, but I do need you to help me to understand why."

"I can't move past this and I'm leaving."

"I want to try and work through things, but I'm going to need some time to process things."

WHAT NEXT? ⟶

The walls of your relationship have come falling down, but that doesn't mean they can't be rebuilt. You have an opportunity here to build a relationship that is stronger, more open, and more connected than ever before. You also have an opportunity to walk away and start anew. Only you will know which one is the right path for you.

You and Your Partner Aren't on the Same Page about Having Kids

If there's ever going to be a deal-breaker, it's this one. If one of you is pining for mini-mes and the other can't think of anything worse than sleepless nights and puréed food, can you reconcile and stay together?

 **Follow these steps to get started:**

1 Be upfront about what you want.
This is one conversation that's worth having before making a serious commitment. Whether you want to have children or not is so divisive that it's best to be totally clear about what you want. Spell out the vision: Is it a big family, one child, absolutely no children, or a "maybe" but you don't want to make any promises?

2 Talk about your fears.
Children are just about the biggest commitment you can ever make. Help your partner to understand what your fears are. Is it that you'll miss the boat and won't ever be able to have the life experiences you want? Or is it that you're worried about losing your freedom? Or how much children cost?

3 Get some practice in.
If one or both of you are on the fence, can you practice caring for children more? Spend more time with friends who've already taken the plunge? Or maybe budget for how you could afford childcare? Help make the idea of having children more of a reality to work out whether it's right for you.

DON'T BANK ON YOUR PARTNER CHANGING THEIR MIND.
This is not one of those areas of your life where holding out and hoping is a smart idea. Part of what makes the kids, or no kids, issue so challenging is the fact that there's a time constraint on it. If your partner is a constant "maybe," soon the pressure might feel cyclonic to get this show on the road. Accept that they won't change their mind, or accept that it's time to move on.

✔ HERE'S HOW

In an ideal world, you would have sat down and had the "what's on your bucket list" chat when you were in the earlier stages of dating. If you're in love with someone who has very different ideas around having children, then enlist a professional to help you talk this through.

Think This:	**Say This:**
"Loving my partner means accepting them—including their views around having children. If we're not on the same page, I need to decide whether that means our relationship has run its course."	"I've actually never seen myself having children, and I don't think I'll ever change my mind."
	"I love you, but having children is something I've always wanted. I accept that we can't do that together, and so I need to find someone who shares that life goal."
	"I accept you totally, and I am happy with the fact that you do [or do not] want kids."

WHAT NEXT? ⟶

If you choose to stay together, remember that you don't have to be a parent to have a connection with children: Become an involved aunt, uncle, or godparent. If you've found yourself exiting a relationship because your partner didn't want kids, it could be empowering for you to explore options to have children independently, as well as look into meeting a new partner.

You Are Having Fertility Issues

There were going to be first-birthday parties, Little League, and a big, cozy family during the holidays. Fast-forward a couple of years, and that just hasn't happened for you. While your friends have seemed to easily become pregnant ("We weren't even trying!"), you and your partner have struggled, and inevitably it's taken a toll on your relationship. How do you stay strong when you're having fertility issues?

 **Follow these steps to get started:**

1 Create an action plan.
Despite best intentions and efforts, whether you conceive or not may come down to chance. To help manage the stress of all the uncertainty, plan for what you can: Have a clear budget in mind for treatment, have an idea of how long you want to try for, and look into contingency options if biological parenthood is off the table.

2 Make sex not about reproduction for a moment.
Trying to make a baby can take the fun out of sex. Maybe you're done with tracking your cycle or having your partner pee on a stick to determine when you have sex. You'll feel like every month counts, but can you have sex again just for fun? Or just to reconnect? Your relationship with one another also needs nurturing.

3 Ask for reassurance.
If you fear that your partner will leave you should the fertility issues be on your part, then you need to annex off this insecurity. Talk about how you're feeling and ask for reassurance. The idea of not having biological children is enough for you to process without the additional anxiety of worrying that your partner is going to leave you too.

DON'T BELIEVE THERE'S ONE RIGHT WAY TO DEAL WITH THIS. Perhaps you want to try again and your partner doesn't. Don't jump to the conclusion that this means they don't care about having children. Instead, this could mean they care very much but are putting your relationship first.

☑ HERE'S HOW

You have to find a way to come back together as a team on this one. You started this journey together, and whatever way it turns out, you want to end it together. Don't let the stress of this period in your life claim your relationship with it. You need to find a halfway point between how you want to handle things (whether that's finding a compromise on how many cycles of IVF you or your partner should have, or how many friends you should open up to). Your relationship isn't a failure because you don't have children (yet).

Think This:	**Say This:**
"And this too shall come to an end." Fertility isn't part of anyone's life forever (except if you're a gynecologist). It is a season in your life when you're focused on having children. Whichever way that journey goes, it won't go on forever. The stress you're experiencing now (no matter how profound) is temporary.	"I love you and our goal of having a family together, but I need to take a pause from this challenge to recharge my emotional batteries." "I want us to make love, and just to focus on being together." "Whatever happens won't change my feelings about you or my desire to be in a committed relationship with you."

WHAT NEXT? ⟶

You can't say whether you will or won't be parents. Yes, you're dealing with a big unknown here, but all relationships will face challenges. Everyone has limited control over what life throws at them, but you do have a choice in your attitude toward these challenges. Babies or no babies, choose each other. Choose to be happy.

Your Relationship Changed Once You Had Kids

You've been up every night this week because little Olivia has a fever. Somehow, this has also synced up with the dishwasher breaking, moving house, and someone misplacing Mr. Snuggles. Did you look in that other box? It's unsurprising in the constant melee that is raising young children that your relationship has changed. Sunday morning sleep-ins and sex marathons have been edged out by early-morning wake-up calls and being on call 24/7, 365 days a year to little people. How can your relationship adapt to parenthood?

 Follow *these steps to get started:*

1 Appreciate your partner.
There's something about staying up all night with a sick toddler so the other partner can get more sleep that's deeply heroic. Sure, it's not a romantic dinner, but in many ways it's a purer gesture of love and care. Let your partner know how much you appreciate them.

2 Ask for help.
Put out a mayday. You need time off. If you're feeling frazzled, and you're having petty arguments with one another, you might just need a few hours to recharge. Move in a grandparent, pay for a sitter, or ask your best friend nicely to take your kids to the park (they'll be fine!).

3 Make sure everyone gets their basic needs met.
Readjust what you consider to be an achievement for the day: If people get to work on time, everyone (except Mr. Snuggles, who really needs a bath) is clean, everyone is fed, and the lights are still on—that's an achievement.

DON'T GET TOO STRESSED IF SEX GOES ONTO THE BACK BURNER. Less sex right now doesn't mean your relationship is broken or can't flourish again; it probably means you're both very, very tired right now. Avoid creating a narrative where your relationship is somehow not good enough. Practice that magical word "acceptance" and trust that things will get back on track in the end.

✓ HERE'S HOW

Yes, your relationship has changed. It's no longer "just the two of us." That doesn't mean, though, that there can't be time for just the two of you. The relationship between you two is more important than ever; the love and commitment you share is the bedrock of your family. If you're not pulling in the same direction, things are going to get difficult. So taking time out for you to reconnect isn't at cross-purposes to being good parents; it's because you want to be good parents that you need time together as a couple.

Think This:

"This isn't forever." You may sometimes wish you could stay in the same moment in time, but relationships always change and grow. Yes, you've left your honeymoon phase behind, but after supporting one another on the journey of parenthood together, you can find a deeper love and mutual respect than was ever possible before.

Say This:

"Thank you for doing this with me. I couldn't ask for a better teammate."

"Let's get a sitter this weekend; we need time out to recharge."

"Go back to bed, I've got this. You need your rest."

WHAT NEXT?

If there's one guarantee, it's that things will change. If you can approach this challenging time with realistic expectations and appreciation for your partner, then you can arrive on the other side of this phase proud of what you've achieved.

You and Your Partner Are Looking to Reconnect Now That Your Kids Are Moved Out

For decades, your lives have been focused on bringing up your kids. Your relationship has taken a back seat to school runs, sick days, and civilizing your children. Now they're adults who know how to look after themselves. It's just the two of you again. How can you reconnect?

 Follow *these steps to get started:*

1 Make a bucket list.
If you look back, there are probably a lot of needs that you put onto the back burner. Pick them up again. Putting yourselves first may seem like an alien concept, but it can also be the start of a brand-new, exciting era. Plan that trip to Europe. Take a Tantra workshop together, or finally get the time you need as an individual to write the book you know is in you.

2 Be irresponsible again.
Rewind the clock twenty years: Remember that person who used to be the last to leave the dance floor? Who had an outrageous dress sense? That's still you. When was the last time you spent all day vegging out in bed? Got tipsy? Made love in the middle of the afternoon? Yes, you'll miss the kids, but they haven't really gone anywhere, and now you both get to go back to developing your relationships with yourselves again.

3 Start a new project.
It could be as simple as taking up a hobby together, or as bold as launching a business. You're good at working as a team. Create a new purpose for yourselves now that you're no longer just parents.

DON'T LONG TOO MUCH FOR THE GOOD OLD DAYS. Yes, the first time your then-five-year-old wrote their list to Santa was magical, but just remember that they also got food poisoning that year. Don't go back through your memories with rose-tinted glasses, and if you do, go back to the ones that are pre-kids. Remember where it all began: a love story between the two of you.

 **HERE'S HOW**

You've experienced another seismic shift in your relationship: Do you notice how they don't let up? Much like a baby's sleep cycles, the moment you think you've got it down pat, everything changes again. So how can you make the most of this new era? Think back to your previous self: Is there a hobby you'd like to try out again? Can you have a planning session with your wider family about how you can make the most of all the time you have now?

Think This:

"We've achieved something special here, what's next?" Don't trick yourself into thinking your work here is done, and now there's nothing left. You need to perform relationship alchemy again and change what it means to be together.

Say This:

"Do you remember when we first met?"

"Those aren't the good old days; these are the good old days."

"Let's finally plan that trip..."

WHAT NEXT? ⟶

Your story is still being written, so make sure this next chapter is a good one. Yes, you've been parents, but can you also be small business owners, avid travelers, or semi-professional tango dancers as well? Most importantly, can you stop calling each other "mom" or "dad" and start investing in your relationship with one another again?

You Are Dealing with an Unexpected Death

Your partnership has stood the test of time (and maybe even some kids), and now you're met with another challenge: Someone close to one, or both, of you has passed away. How do you support one another when you deal with grief in different ways? How can you ride the waves of sadness, despair, and anger together until you reach a new normal?

 *Follow these steps to get started:*

1 Be patient.
Grief can appear in strange ways. Your partner might feel lethargic one minute and furious the next, while you become anxious about your own health. It will be an emotional roller coaster. Right now probably feels like one step forward, two steps back, but hold on to the fact (with the right support) that it won't always be this way. Be patient and give things time.

2 Seek professional support.
One person can only handle so much. If you're torn between supporting your partner, looking after your kids, holding down a job, and navigating this difficult time, that's a lot. You and your partner will benefit from having a professional therapist or counselor to share your feelings with and gain reassurance from.

3 Get support for yourself.
Every caregiver needs a caregiver. Your partner may be physically well, but if their mental health has taken a backslide since the news, you will also need help helping them. This could mean you lean more on friends and family for support, or you enlist one of their friends to take them out for the day to give you headspace. Share the burden throughout your network.

DON'T BECOME TOO FRUSTRATED WITH YOUR PARTNER.
It will be hard, and you may even feel guilty for not having bound-less empathy, but if all the chores, childcare, and emotional stability suddenly fall on your shoulders, it will take its toll. Do your best to recognize when you need help—before you snap. Don't feel guilty about needing some time out or extra help around the house to get through this period.

✓ HERE'S HOW

Your and/or your partner's grief won't exactly pass (do you ever get over a fundamental loss?), but with professional support, it should mellow into feelings that are more manageable for you both. Accept that this is going to be a testing time, and don't hold back on hitting the "mayday!" button to get extra support yourself. Keep listening, even if your and/or your partner's feelings seem to change on an hourly basis, and know this, too, shall pass.

Think This:	**Say This:**
"My needs, and our relationship, are on the back burner right now and that doesn't always feel good. I miss how we were before this happened, but I also have faith that we will get back to better days. For now I'm going to let go of any feelings of resentment that I can and ask for all the support that I also need."	"It's okay; you're allowed to feel how you feel."
	"Would you be able to spend time with [partner] this weekend so I can have a rest?"
	"You won't feel this way forever."

WHAT NEXT?

Your partnership might be tested right now, but with love and dedication you can get through it. If your or your partner's mental health continues to decline, seek ongoing professional support and treatment. Take care of your own needs as best as you can, and reassure yourself that this challenging time is finite.

You Need to Discuss What Will Happen If One of You Dies

"Life is made of first meetings and final partings." They say all good things must come to an end, but it can feel deeply uncomfortable when the end of life becomes a reality. Whether one of you is facing a terminal prognosis, or you've gotten to a stage in life where planning for the future becomes essential, here's how you can approach this difficult subject with pragmatism and compassion.

 Follow *these steps to get started:*

1 **Start planning now.**
If you have dependent children or are in a life partnership where you don't wish to legally marry, then now is a good time to put together an end-of-life plan. If you're unmarried, things can be legally more complex, particularly if you have children. To make sure your significant other is treated by law as if they were your spouse, you'll want to put a will in place. Life insurance can be a helpful safety net if one of you is the main breadwinner.

2 **Have an end-of-life care plan.**
If you're terminally ill or have strong preferences about care in the event of illness, think ahead to what care you'd like to receive. In the event you become less able to make decisions or articulate them, this will help you to express your wishes for medical treatment in advance.

3 **Get professional help or consult a leader of your faith community.**
It will take time to come to terms with an end-of-life plan. This is a huge burden to take on as a couple. Take outside support from a professional or spiritual leader who is used to guiding people through this life stage.

DON'T FEEL THERE'S ONE RIGHT WAY TO APPROACH THIS; IT IS ABOUT HONORING YOUR OR YOUR PARTNER'S PREFERENCES. Creating a box of memories or a video series for your loved ones after your passing can be a nice thing to do, but it's equally valid for you to want to stay present and not participate in that way.

 HERE'S HOW

As difficult as conversations about end of life are, you or your partner may find it comforting to have a plan in place. Knowing that all the practical arrangements are tied up and that you don't have to worry about financial provisions for your family in the event of your or your partner's death can be comforting. Start an ongoing conversation (maybe with the help of a professional) about both of your choices, and put a plan in place that honors your personal preferences.

Think This:	**Say This:**
"I find these conversations difficult, but I accept this is something we have to plan for, and I will help support my partner through this too."	"Your choices are valid." "It might feel like a long way off, but let's get some practical steps in place in the event either of us passes." "I want to help make sure your wishes are made clear."

WHAT NEXT? ⟶

This final step of parting is one no one wants to take. It's easier just to pretend it doesn't have to happen, right? But in helping to have a clear plan for the future, you will make it (or at least the practical decisions that lie ahead) easier to face.

You Don't Like Your Partner's Family, and They Don't Like You

You wish you got along with your in-laws, but you don't, and the feeling is more than mutual. Maybe they spoil your sister-in-law's grandkids and ignore yours, or have a dysfunctional relationship with your partner that you're sick of being dragged into. You wish your partner would stand up to them, but they don't, and you're not sure you can keep the peace much longer.

 **Follow these steps to get started:**

1 Recognize that families are for life.
This is probably the best argument for why you should really try to invest in this relationship, even if you don't want to. They're not going anywhere! Even if you don't feel like they meet you halfway, make an effort: Join in their family traditions, turn up on time for gatherings, and express how you were looking forward to seeing them.

2 Let go of expectations.
You might struggle to understand why no one stepped in to help after your child was born, or why your mother-in-law is obsessive about you making your bed during a long visit, but each family is different. The mental playbook you have for family life has come from your own upbringing; try not to see your partner's family as "not as good" just because they are different.

3 Accept that it takes time for you (and your children) to integrate.
When a new significant partner joins the family, or a new grandkid is thrown into the mix, everyone has to find their new place in the family. Understand that everyone learning how to share resources will take a bit of time when a new family member is added.

DON'T LEAVE THE HIGH GROUND. It can be very challenging to tell your partner *exactly* what you think of their family (particularly if you feel they haven't been kind to your children; your inner bear rage will come out!). However, even if you really, really don't like your in-laws, avoid running them down in front of your partner. Express your feelings, sure, but do it in a mature and dignified way.

HERE'S HOW

Create reasonable boundaries to help yourself to cope. If you (hand on heart!) don't think you'll ever be able to get along with them, then think about what you need to help yourself be calm and accepting of your in-laws. Is it that you limit stays at their house to one weekend maximum? Stay in a separate hotel on the annual family vacation to have some personal space? Think about what you need to continue being the reasonable, diplomatic in-law that you are.

Think This:	Say This:
"I find my relationship with my partner's family very challenging. However, I ultimately accept that they are my family too. We might never be close, but hopefully over time we can find ways to relate to one another better."	"We should go and watch your nephew's soccer match. It would mean a lot to him." "I know the family holiday is important, but can we agree to have separate accommodations so I can get some breathing space?" "We don't always see eye to eye, but they're your family, so I will always love and accept them."

WHAT NEXT?

There's a long runway to get to know these relatives. Be open to the possibility that mutual respect could grow out of dislike for one another. Your in-laws are your family too.

You're Dealing with Your Partner's Ex

Perhaps your partner and their ex share children, and your plans always come second to their family commitments. Or maybe it's that the specter of their ex haunts your conversations—why is it that they keep comparing you to them? How do you form a strong relationship when their ex is still a part of their life?

 Follow these steps to get started:

1 Consider whether they are not over their ex, or you feel insecure.
If you think that they're still hung up on their ex, don't just have selective hearing. Don't torture yourself by focusing on the limited details you know about their relationship with their ex; focus on how they're treating you.

2 Reflect on how open they are about their past relationship.
Far fewer red flags are raised if a friendship with an ex is out in the open. If it's been a given from the start of your relationship that they're still friends, or if they share children, this is a part of their life to be accepted. Be more wary if they've concealed ongoing contact with an ex.

3 Think carefully about what you can accept.
If someone has children, then you will often have to make compromises. If that romantic minibreak you planned clashes with the weekend that they have the kids, prepare to give way. If that level of compromise is unacceptable to you, then you may need to find a partner with fewer commitments. Likewise, if your partner is still in touch with an ex, think about what level of contact (if any) feels right to you. If you're okay sending them a happy birthday message, but feel uncomfortable about them meeting up one-on-one for dinner, verbalize those boundaries.

DON'T ASSUME YOUR PARTNER IS CHEATING. People stay in touch with their exes for all sorts of reasons: They can't let go, they've become good friends, they're close to their ex's sister.... Don't assume the worst when you discover your partner is in touch with an ex; talk to them instead.

 HERE'S HOW

There is no gold-standard rule for how to deal with an ex who's still in the picture. You may need to accept that they have ongoing commitments with their ex. You may need to identify what you're not comfortable with, and communicate that. You may need to ask for more reassurance, because your insecurities are getting the better of you.

Think This:	**Say This:**
"I'm not going to assume that them being in touch with their ex means that they're being unfaithful. I'm going to talk to them about it and keep an open mind. I won't let my insecurities get the better of me or push me to jump to conclusions."	"I'm disappointed you can't make it, but I do understand that your commitment to your children comes first." "I want to understand why it's important to you to stay in touch with your ex." "The past is the past, and I know there's a reason why that relationship didn't work out."

WHAT NEXT?

Exes are exes for a reason. If the relationship your partner and their ex shared was perfect, your partner wouldn't be with you today. Work toward having high self-worth and avoid comparing yourself to your partner's ex.

You're Missing Your Ex

Your relationship is really good, except for one small snag: The past keeps coming back to haunt you. You find yourself thinking about your ex. Okay, you're still in touch with your ex, and if you're honest with yourself, perhaps you're not quite over them yet? You can't help but compare your new partner to how things were in the past. Will you ever feel the same way about your current partner as you did about them?

 *Follow these steps to get started:*

1 **Honestly reflect on why you are still in touch.**
This might sound like an easy question ("We've been friends for ages!"), but make sure you dig a little deeper to get to the truth. Exes can become great friends, but sometimes that relationship is less about friendship and more about control. You (or they) just can't quite let go. What needs are you meeting by staying in touch with a former partner?

2 **Write down ten reasons why it would not have worked with your ex.**
Challenge yourself to focus on what it was actually like being in a relationship with your ex. Forget about that romantic kiss in the snow, and start remembering all the times they let you down, or simply demonstrated that you weren't compatible.

3 **Accept some reasonable boundaries here.**
Would your partner like to meet your ex if you're that good of "friends"? Would they expect you to have called them instead of your ex when you got stuck? For your current relationship to flourish there may be some boundaries that need to be put into place.

DON'T PRETEND THAT YOUR PREVIOUS RELATIONSHIP WAS PERFECT. Yes, perhaps your ex was more romantic, but did that come at a price of them being emotionally unavailable? Have you conveniently forgotten about all the bad things about your relationship? Avoid comparing the day-to-day reality of your current relationship with the highlights reel of your ex.

 # HERE'S HOW

An ex in the background can be a great fall guy for insecurities about your relationship. If you're not 100 percent sure about your partner, or you've had an argument, a sympathetic ex standing by can ensure that all your emotional eggs aren't in one basket. If this is you, be realistic about what your motivations are, and recognize that you can't offset your fear of intimacy with having someone on the back burner forever.

Think This:

"I want my partner to feel secure in our relationship, so I'm going to be open and inclusive about the friendship I share with my ex. If I feel reluctant to share those details, then I will be honest with myself that there's another agenda at play here beyond just friendship."

Say This:

"We worked out that we were much better as friends. It would be great to set up a time for you to meet them."

"I acknowledge I've been holding on to that relationship for too long and I need to let it go."

"I want you to feel really secure in our relationship."

WHAT NEXT?

Focus less on the ex and more on what your tie to them is telling you about the relationship between you and your current partner. Is there a need you're not getting met in your current relationship that means you're always reaching out to your ex? Don't get too distracted by the ex thing; there are the bigger questions about your relationship that you need to ask yourself.

You're Not Feeling Appreciated by Your Partner

You remember your anniversary, do tons of laundry, and still make an effort on date night, but you're starting to feel underappreciated. It's like no matter how many good deeds you do, your partner nitpicks on minor imperfections or simply doesn't even notice you exist. How do you cope when you're not feeling appreciated by your partner?

 Follow *these steps* *to get started:*

1 Consider whether they show that they care in other ways.
If you're not feeling appreciated, does your partner show you that they care with deeds instead of words? While you may never get told that they like your haircut, are they a superstar at putting the trash out?

2 Stop over-giving.
If you're running yourself down, picking up more than your fair share of the chores, just stop. You might panic ("But then it will never get done!"), but if you constantly over-give and never communicate that you are feeling overstretched, there's no opportunity for your partner to change their behavior. Ask for what you need to be calm and happy. Even if you're not sure that they'll listen to you, it's better to at least try to communicate, rather than stockpiling resentment.

3 Reflect on whether there is a deeper issue here.
Is your partner always nit-picking? Or are they emotionally abusive? Is nothing you do ever good enough? Are you trying to be perfect out of fear that your partner will snatch away their affection if you put a foot out of place? All couples bicker from time to time, but make sure your relationship is a net positive, rather than one that's emotionally abusive.

DON'T RETALIATE; INSTEAD COMMUNICATE. If you keep doing nice things for your partner that go unnoticed, there can be a temptation to enter into passive-aggressive behavior. They didn't notice that you did their laundry again? You sulk. If you find yourself withdrawing when they don't notice something nice you did, sit your partner down and make them aware of how you're feeling.

 **HERE'S HOW**

Start to regain your independence, and don't be totally reliant on your partner's praise to feel good about yourself. Of course everyone wants their partner's love and affection; however, your partner can't be the only person in your life who makes you feel appreciated. If your relationship is feeling stale to the point where you're not sure if your partner even notices you're there anymore, do more to nourish your independence. Go out with friends instead of doing the ironing one night. Pick up a book you love rather than sitting in silence watching the TV. Go out for a run on Sunday morning instead of cooking brunch for everyone. Bump your own needs up the priority list.

Think This:	**Say This:**
"I'm not going to withdraw or feel emotionally wounded by the fact that they haven't noticed how much I'm giving to this relationship; instead I'm going to ask for what I need."	"I need some me-time this weekend, so would you be okay taking the kids to soccer practice this time?" "I really like it when you compliment me like that." "I know this probably isn't your intention, but I do sometimes feel overlooked in our relationship."

WHAT NEXT? ⟶

Have you asked for what you need? Have you stopped over-giving? Have you put your own needs first and not felt bad about it? If you feel your partner no longer appreciates you, reinvigorate your independence.

RESOURCE LIST

BOOKS

The 5 Love Languages: The Secret to Love That Lasts by Gary Chapman

Eight Dates: Essential Conversations for a Lifetime of Love by John Gottman

Attached: Are You Anxious, Avoidant or Secure? by Amir Levine and Rachel S.F. Heller

Mating in Captivity: Unlocking Erotic Intelligence by Esther Perel

The State of Affairs: Rethinking Infidelity by Esther Perel

Gaslighting: Recognize Manipulative and Emotionally Abusive People—and Break Free by Stephanie Moulton Sarkis

Alonement: How to Be Alone & Absolutely Own It by Francesca Specter

PODCASTS

Jillian Michaels: Keeping It Real

www.jillianmichaels.com/podcast/ shape-your-love-life-dating-coach- hayley-quinn?language_content_ entity=en

Katherine Ryan: Telling Everybody Everything

https://podcasts.apple .com/gb/podcast/match- bonus-episode-on-dating/ id1507148315?i=1000514473903

The Emma Guns Show

https://shows.acast.com/ emmagunavardhana/episodes/the- easy-scienceofdatingwithhayleyquinn

SOCIAL MEDIA

Hayley Quinn: YouTube

www.youtube.com/c/HayleyQuinn

Hayley Quinn: *Instagram*

www.instagram.com/hayleyquinnx/

VIDEOS

Hayley Quinn: TEDx Talk—"Searching for Love to Escape Ourselves"

www.youtube.com/
watch?v=jmUayKnHWWM&t=21s

Hayley Quinn: Live Coaching Videos on Match

https://uk.match.com/p/
video-coaching/

DATING WEBSITES AND BLOGS

***Hayley Quinn* website**

www.hayleyquinn.com

Hayley Quinn: Dating Coach for Men

www.hayleyquinn.com/men

Hayley Quinn: Dating Coach for Women

www.hayleyquinn.com/women

Hayley Quinn Club

https://hayleyquinnclub.com

Hayley Quinn: Single Parent Dating Tips

https://blog.frolo.com/2021/04/21/
single-parent-dating-tips/

The Gottman Institute: A Research-Based Approach to Relationships

www.gottman.com

Matchmaking with Vida Consultancy

https://maclynninternational.us/

Sarrah Rose: Tantric Activation (Sex & Relationships for Men)

https://tantricactivation.com/

RELATIONSHIP COUNSELING

www.healthline.com/health/mental-
health/therapy-for-couples (US)

www.relate.org.uk (UK)

MONEY MANAGEMENT

www.moneysavingexpert.com

BUYING A HOUSE AS A COUPLE

www.forbes.com/advisor/mortgages/
buying-a-house-unmarried/ (US)

www.experian.com/blogs/ask-
experian/how-to-buy-a-house-with-
someone-youre-not-married-to (US)

https://hoa.org.uk/advice/guides-for-homeowners/i-am-buying/buying-a-home-with-a-partner-or-friend-what-to-watch-for/ (UK)

DEALING WITH BEREAVEMENT

www.helpguide.org/articles/grief/coping-with-grief-and-loss.htm

CHRONOTYPES

www.sleepfoundation.org/how-sleep-works/chronotypes

DOMESTIC ABUSE SERVICES

https://ncadv.org/get-help (US)

www.nhs.uk/live-well/healthy-body/getting-help-for-domestic-violence/ (UK)

LEGAL AID FOR HELP WITH RESTRAINING ORDERS

www.thehotline.org/get-help/domestic-violence-legal-help/ (US)

www.womenagainstabuse.org/services/legal-center (US)

www.gov.uk/legal-aid/domestic-abuse-or-violence (UK)

https://childlawadvice.org.uk/information-pages/legal-aid-if-you-have-been-a-victim-of-domestic-abuse-or-violence/ (UK)

www.womensaid.org.uk/the-survivors-handbook/your-legal-rights/ (UK)

PARENTING RESOURCES

www.apa.org/monitor/2018/04/parenting-resources

www.familyeducation.com/family-life/nontraditional-families

https://thestorkandi.com

ADOPTION RESOURCES

https://adoption.com/ (US)

www.americanadoptions.com (US)

www.adoptionuk.org (UK)

INFERTILITY RESOURCES

https://resolve.org/get-help/helpful-resources-and-advice/managing-infertility-stress/coping-techniques/

www.verywellfamily.com/coping-with-infertility-how-to-feel-better-1959979

LIFE INSURANCE RESOURCES

www.gocompare.com/life-insurance/

LAST WILL RESOURCES

https://meetfabric.com/blog/how-to-write-a-last-will-and-testament (US)

www.gov.uk/make-will (UK)

INDEX

187

ABOUT THE AUTHOR

Hayley Quinn is an international dating coach who empowers men and women to learn to love dating. From her popular TEDx Talk to radio and TV appearances on BBC News and *Celebs Go Dating*, her goal is to help people feel confident and meet the people they deserve. She is the spokesperson for *Match UK*, one of the largest online dating sites in the world, and her work has been featured on *Elle*, *Match*, *Cosmopolitan*, and more. She has also written the rom-com novel *The Last First Date*. Learn more at HayleyQuinn.com.

PREPARE FOR A SUCCESSFUL CAREER

Learn What to Do (and What NOT to Do) in the Workplace!